NOTES FROM CHINA

NOTES
FROM
CHINA

—— BY ——

Barbara W. Tuchman

COLLIER BOOKS

NEW YORK

Notes I through VIII were originally written for and distributed by The Associated Press.

Note IX, "Friendship with Foreign Devils," is reprinted by permission of *Harper's Magazine* and appeared in the December 1972 issue.

"If Mao Had Come to Washington in 1945: An Essay in Alternatives" is reprinted by permission from *Foreign Affairs,* October 1972.

The Macmillan Company
866 Third Avenue, New York, N.Y. 10022
Collier-Macmillan Canada Ltd., Toronto, Ontario

Library of Congress Catalog Card Number: 72–93468

FIRST COLLIER BOOKS EDITION 1972

PRINTED IN THE UNITED STATES OF AMERICA

Contents

(Illustrations between pages 50 and 51)

Photographs by Barbara and Alma Tuchman

A Note on
How I Came to China

THIS is what I vowed I would never do—put ephemeral journalism between the covers of a book. But I was offered a persuasive rationale: that these reports are the outcome not only of a six-week visit but of an interest in the Far East that goes back almost forty years.

In 1933 on graduating from college, I joined the staff of the American Council of the Institute of Pacific Relations, an international organization representing countries with territory on the Pacific. In October 1934 I went to Tokyo for a year's stay to work on a project of the IPR, *The Economic Handbook of the Pacific Area*. It was the hope of the Institute, by centering the work in Tokyo, to keep contact with and possibly encourage the liberal elements in Japan, but controlling tendencies there proved to be in another direction. In October 1935 I went home by way of China where I visited Peking and the vicinity for about a month and continued on via the Trans-Siberian Railroad.

My first published work grew out of this year in the Far East. It included an article for the IPR quarterly on the Russo-Japanese fisheries for which I was paid $30, the first money I ever earned by writing; a review of *Tsushima,* a vivid history of the decisive battle of the Russo-Japanese War, a book I still remember well; and a little essay on the Japanese character which, to the astonishment of its unknown twenty-three-year-old author, made its way onto the imposing pages, alongside prime ministers, world bankers, and other pontiffs, of *Foreign Affairs.*

After a seven-year interval (focused on the Spanish Civil War and the menace of Hitler) my brief experience of Asia earned me a place on the Far East desk of the Office of War Information during World War II. As I was married with a child by this time, I stayed in the New York office whose operations were beamed to the allied and occupied countries of Europe. For the Far East desk it was a chronic battle against the Europe-oriented staff to get news of the war in Asia on the air at all. (Correspondents in China and Japan in the 1930s similarly fought to get their dispatches into print against the disinterest of editors and presumably of the public. I once accompanied an enterprising correspondent when he hired a number of Japanese laborers to wash down the great Buddha of Kamakura so that he could take pictures and write a story about the Buddha's supposed ceremonial bath.) At OWI we gained a place for the Far East news only because it was one of the aims of the operation to explain to our allies why so much American effort was engaged in the Pacific.

Since missionaries' sons and serious students of Asia were all snapped up by OSS and OWI for assignments in the field, or in the Washington office where policy was made, I was one of the few staff members in New York with a personal if minuscule knowledge of the Far East. I was dragged out of bed to write the backgrounder on Tokyo on the night of our first long-range bomber attack in 1944 (for which no one had prepared). I wrote the backgrounders on the East China coast for the landing that never came, and on the Soviet Far East for the Russian entry against Japan that came only five days before the end. For some weeks I even took over the Indo-China desk in the absence of its normal occupant because, on the strength of a research paper I had once done for the IPR, I was the only person in the office who could say Laos, Cambodia, Cochin-China, Tonkin, Annam (the five states of Indo-China; no one then had ever heard of Vietnam) without hesitating.

For a while I also covered the Burma campaign in acrimonious rivalry with the military desk which considered Burma their turf while we at FE considered it ours. It was in the course of defending this territory that I followed the exploits of and became interested in General Stilwell. During the next twenty years the interest receded but remained a flickering ember that never died.

Meanwhile the restoration of the state of Israel after a gap of nearly 2,000 years struck me as an event unique in history and started me on my first book, *Bible and Sword*. Ending with the Balfour Declaration of 1918, this led me to *The Zimmermann Telegram* of 1917 which in turn led back to 1914 and *The Guns of August*, and that in turn to the social origins of the Great War in *The Proud Tower*. By the time that book was published, it was 1966. The American relation to Asia was now an importunate reality. No one needed to wash Buddhas to get it into the press.

Stilwell revived in my mind from a combination of reasons: because it offered what I had long been looking for, an important body of unpublished papers to work from; because his career made an ideal focus for a book on the American relation to China; and because when I discussed the subject with my eldest daughter and son-in-law, two highly educated, cosmopolitan young people, I was struck by the fact that they knew nothing about America's past connection with China, but wanted to know. When I proposed an alternative subject that I had in mind at the time, they insisted that I must do the book on China, so I did.

I first approached the Stilwell family for access to the Papers in March 1967. *Stilwell and the American Experience in China, 1911–45*, was published in February 1971 two months before China opened its doors to the American Ping-Pong team, with Henry Kissinger not far behind. I can hardly claim to have foreseen this turn of events, much less its fortunate coincidence for my book, but when people ask how did I happen to choose China, I like to suggest that if a historian understands the past he will have acquired in the process a feel of the future.

China was closed to Americans during the time I was writing the book, but though it was now too late for that purpose, I applied for a visa out of the intense interest my task had aroused in me. While waiting for a response I wrote the essay for *Foreign Affairs* that forms the second section of this book. In June 1972 I received word that I was invited to visit China. The journey was made in company with my youngest daughter, Alma, over a period of six weeks in July and August.

The *Notes* appear as originally written, under some pressure. I have made no revisions except to erase the erratic editing that afflicted them in some newspapers, notably *The New York Times*. Somewhere in that institution is a copy editor whose idea of meaningful prose remains an enigma.

NOTES FROM CHINA

I

Standing Up

IN a country where misery and want were the foundation of the social structure, famine was periodic, death from starvation common, disease pervasive, thievery normal, and graft and corruption taken for granted, the elimination of these conditions in Communist China is so striking that negative aspects of the new rule fade in relative importance. The dominant fact is that for China's working class, which is to say over 80 percent of the world's most populous country, the lid of exploitation has been lifted. While visible betterment varies widely between the major cities and the provinces, it is probably true to say of all areas that the working class, in whose interest China is now governed, have found a sense of purpose, self-confidence, and dignity in the knowledge that they are the object of the state's concern, not, as in the past, society's victims.

The most obvious negative in the process is the mental monotone imposed upon the country. All thought, all ideas past, present, and future, not to mention the historic record, are twisted, manipulated, rolled out, and flattened into one, expressed in half a dozen slogans dinned incessantly and insistently into the heads of the public. As far as the life of the mind in China is concerned, its scope has rigid limits and its sound is a blaring, endlessly repeated single note, with effect (at least upon a Westerner) like the drip, drip, drip on the victim's head of the ancient Chinese water torture—if it had made a loud noise. The message is that "the People" are the motive force; that Marxism-Leninism is universal truth, and that propelled by its principles and Chairman Mao's thought, China's working class can ultimately build Socialism, meaning well-being for everyone. The goal lies ahead and can only be reached by keeping the Revolution green, that is by continually renewed contact with the masses.

Domestically it seems to work. I say "seems" throughout these notes cautiously and advisedly because ignorance of the language is a barrier equal to being deaf. A six-week visitor under this handicap can offer conclusions as impressions only.

Perhaps too the transfer to collectivism has been made easier because China's life was in some ways collective to begin with. Consider the *kang*, the built-in wall-to-wall bed of north China on which, in the poorer homes, the whole family sleeps. With that in their background, collective adjustment is natural, not to say imperative.

In any event, from what we could see through eleven cities (Peking, Taiyuan, Yenan, Sian, Loyang, Chengchow, Wuhan, Nanking, Suchow,

4

Shanghai, and Canton) and a variety of rural settlements, collective effort has made up China's oldest lack—enough food. Our reception at an agricultural commune in central Shansi included three or four heaping platters each of sliced tomatoes, fresh peaches, and sweetened stuffed dumplings made of glutinous rice (a substance to make a Western stomach quail) in far greater abundance than was required by the company. Admittedly this was laid on to impress the visitors (as was everything else we met in China), but the availability of such abundance to agricultural workers and their un-hungry attitude toward it were simply not possible in the past when, as one member of the commune said, "The lower peasants could not even have the chaff of the rice to eat."

Increased production, materially speaking, is what China's revolution is all about. It refutes all the firm statements of economists and agronomists in the past that China's arable land could not be augmented, nor the yield per unit of land be raised sufficiently to feed the expanding population. Both have been done, not by magic but because the people have been mobilized and motivated to do it—by expropriation and redistribution of land permitting communal farming in large tracts instead of fractional plots, and by the knowledge that everything they do to make improvements will now benefit themselves not the landlord.

I will cite no statistics on increased yield because

5

I cannot judge their reliability, but in this summer's drought in north China with day after relentless day of no rain and of temperatures over 100, when one sees fresh water being pumped in life-giving gushes from irrigation channels, and sees surrounding fields green, vegetables ripening, and seedling crops sprouting instead of withering, one needs no statistics. In the old days this year's drought would have been lethal. The great Miyun Dam and Reservoir northeast of Peking, the pumping stations and sedimentation plants along the Yellow River that have at last harnessed "China's Sorrow," and similar projects constructed elsewhere under the new regime, besides providing hydroelectric power, have brought drought, flood, and famine under control. The result provides the agricultural surplus which, paid in kind to the state as a form of tax, supplies the capital for expansion of industry—the other of the two legs on which the new China walks.

In human terms the process has produced a new person—the worker from the ranks who can become manager of the enterprise. It is true that such people do not bear sole responsibility. They function in committee in a three-in-one arrangement of workers, technicians, and "cadres" or representatives of the Government. Even so, in their straightforward look-you-in-the-eye greeting, their poise and self-respect, they are impressive, none more so than the woman Vice-Chairman of the Revolution-

6

ary Committee of the Szu Tzi Ching (Evergreen) Commune outside Peking.

Quiet, composed, and supremely assured, with bobbed hair, neat overblouse, loose trousers, and a big silver wristwatch, she knew every aspect of the operation: the crop rotation, marketing, fertilizing, spraying, trucking, livestock, the schools, clinics, and family lives of a commune of 6,000 acres and 41,000 people, formerly scattered in hopeless division in 138 villages. Born in a family in the "poor peasant" category, that is, hired or tenant farmers without land of their own, she was now playing a competent role where formerly she had no stake. Her colleague in charge of the orchards, a rough peasant with stubble of beard and sweat towel around his neck, had the same assured air, as did the girl supervisor of the pig sties. Both shook hands with confident equality and exhibited their domains with pride (each ripening peach on the trees was individually bagged and each pig had its own pen).

Their counterparts in industry—like the shop foreman whose intense pride is almost tangible as he watches a finished tractor leave the assembly plant—are equally forthright and precise, in notable contrast to civil servants who, being more vulnerable to the swings and switchbacks of official policy, try to be utterly orthodox and noncommittal to the point of speechlessness.

Obviously the commune and tractor plant were

selected showplaces, but the fact that they exist at all and are managed in part by their workers is a piece of one of the greatest bootstrap operations in history. There have been harsh costs and there are negative aspects, but in these worker-managers China has visibly, to quote who else but the Chairman, "stood up."

II

The People

WHO are "the People," the subject and object of every political slogan in China? According to Chairman Mao's definition, "the People" are all who support the Revolution (dutifully said to be 90 to 95 percent). The remainder, consisting of "class enemies," "bad elements," and counter-revolutionaries, are merely Citizens. This strikes me as a murky Thought, not one of the Chairman's best, or else a poor translation, but since it is the official translation, it will have to stand. Theoretically and ideally, then, the People are a mystic whole (leaving aside the bad elements), but in practice class origin is determining.

Workers, peasants, and soldiers are automatically People (although sometimes they are exhorted to "learn from the People," which is confusing) as is anyone of "poor and lower middle peasant" or other working-class family. Those who come from landlord, rich peasant, merchant-capitalist, or bourgeois origin are automatically out, or at least not full members of society until they have proved by deed and attitude that they have repudiated their class values and wholeheartedly adopted Chairman Mao's "correct revolutionary line" of service to the People. What this requires in outward conformity for those with inner reservations can only be conjectured.

The masses (and for China the word is appropriate in a descriptive, not necessarily Marxist, sense), pedaling unhurriedly to work on their millions of bicycles through the city streets, filling the now public parks of the Imperial City and Summer Palace, crowding a department store or a museum exhibit of People's Art, queueing at cooked food shops for a meal in a bowl, appear quite at ease. The economic security of food, paid work, and old-age pension is a great relaxer of tension, and this appears in faces and manner. China has never been in a hurry, and the pace, even in factory work, is still easy-going. There is no sense of pressure or tension in the air.

A foreigner feels safe (though not comfortable) walking alone anywhere at any time—if he can put up with attracting crowds of intense starers. In the countryside and provincial cities he also attracts smiles and spontaneous handclapping and almost never a scowl, for the Chinese are an agreeable and normally friendly people. Mrs. Chang Si-lan, a tiny spry lady in black whose two-room home (for a family of eight) we visited in a factory compound, welcomed us with such genuine delight that we fell into instant communication. It appeared that she and I were the same age: I pointed to my gray hair while hers was still black; she pointed to her absent teeth while I still had mine. She pressed us to sit beside her on the *kang*, passed cigarettes, and compared grandchildren. On Mrs. Chang's level the Chinese do not insist on talking in ritual fatuities.

Decorum is the word for the masses in the capital. Even more notable, in comparison to former times, is their remarkable appearance of health and well-being, though more so in Peking than in the provinces. The running nose of children, that endemic companion of poverty, has vanished, at least in the main cities. There are no cripples, no beggars, no open sores or disease, although hawking and spitting (outside Peking) are as bad as ever. Even Mao Tse-tung Thought has found no formula to prevail over that.

Opium-smoking, prostitution, and venereal disease have proved easier to eradicate, and according to claims have been wiped out. I cannot vouch for the claim but I can say that any overt interest in sex is simply nonexistent. When the subject came up in conversation with one female interpreter, it produced a grimace of disgust as if we had mentioned a cockroach, and the same expression contorted the face of a doctor of mental health when he was asked about perversions and homosexuality. "We don't have this in China," he replied succinctly.

At a military barracks we visited outside Nanking I noticed no provision for families. The state pays for an officer's home leave or for visits by his family to the post, I was told, but apart from that he does without a wife's companionship. After an officer has served fifteen years and "has a good record," he may apply to have his family live with him. To make sure I had this piece of startling information right, it was repeated for me and confirmed as true for the Army as a whole (although I suspect regional commands vary). When I ventured the comment that this must be a very monastic life, the officer replied, "We consider it a very happy life to live and work with our friends and comrades of the great proletarian People's Liberation Army." That is the way they really talk. (It should be added that the PLA has played a genuinely constructive role in the state which, considering the past role of soldiery in Chinese society, is a revolution in itself; but that is another matter.)

At a May 7th Cadre School deep in the country where bureaucrats and professionals come for a six-month term to be "re-educated" through manual labor, the experience was also celibate. Although they dislike any reference to the question, the Committee was willing to say that their members were too busy with field labor, brick-making, and building (which in fact was hard real work, not leaf-raking) to worry about their sex life. Sex was sublimated in the "struggle for production" and for renewed "revolutionary consciousness." It was the stock answer to be expected, but it is quite possible it may also be true. Whatever the truth, it is evident that in the new society the sex impulse has been pushed deep below the visible surface.

The effect on the family life of the "cadre" class is cooling. (This ubiquitous and absurd word, pronounced "cadder" by Chinese-speaking English— *gan bou* in Chinese—is as basic in Communist usage as "peasant." Originally adopted to mean a government or party bureaucrat, it now loosely covers anyone in an administrative, professional, intellectual, or white-collar job, in short, everyone who is not worker, peasant, or soldier. There is a sharp distinction between lower-echelon cadres called "staff members" and the upper-echelon "leading cadre" who is a person in a position of authority: a minister, bureau chief, manager, director, or head of any organization, except that in theory no one is head because everything is run by committee. The "leading cadre" in each case is Vice-Chairman of the relevant Revolutionary Committee. Perhaps in deference to Number One, a chairman is either nonexistent or never appears.)

As regards family life, many of the cadre class are now confining themselves to one child or two and appear to maintain a rather detached marital relationship. Two of the various escorts who accompanied us at different places and who had working wives or husbands, sent their four-year-old children to boarding kindergarten from which the child comes home only for the one-day weekend. The first of these parents explained airily that "a child at home can be a nuisance, you know." A third had a more surprising solution: her four-year-old son was cared for at home by what she first described as a "roommate," and only at my evident bewilderment reluctantly confessed was a housemaid! I felt myself dangerously in the presence of Revisionism.

This attitude has not yet spread downward, for in the life of the streets, which is the life of the masses, babies and small children are cared for and carried around by brothers and sisters, parents and grandparents (in particular the grandfather); not in the backpack arrangement with head nodding used by the Japanese but cradled in a front-carry which is certainly less efficient but more affectionate.

Among the cadre class, however, homemaking, like child care, is de-emphasized. To eliminate the trouble of cooking, a working couple may often take their meals, including the evening meal, at the office cafeteria, the wife at her office and the husband at his.

The job unit governs the cadre's life, assigns housing, and determines political reliability and periods of May 7th "re-education" if required. More often than not, one is told, the subject volunteers for this experience, perhaps because he considers it the advisable thing to do or because he sincerely wants to renew his Marxist fervor (believed to atrophy in office jobs) through realistic manual labor, as well as to obey the Chairman's order to "combine theory with practice." At one May 7th labor camp for "leading cadres" in the Shensi hills not far from Yenan, the mood seemed positive and the members genuinely and vigorously engaged in outdoor labor under the blazing sun. But the sad, subdued look and remote eyes of a gray-haired surgeon from the leading hospital of the provincial capital suggest that the process does not always work.

In contrast is the provincial political boss, generally designated Vice-Chairman of the Provincial Revolutionary Committe, who may or may not combine in his person the all-powerful office of Party Secretary for the municipality or region. These are hard, beefy men, something between Mike Quill and Khrushchev, whom we came to call the Commissars. From what answers we could elicit, they came mostly from the PLA or had an Army background, and no doubt represented the Army men sent in by Mao to regain control of provincial government after the frenzy of the Cultural Revolution of 1966–69.

We made the acquaintance of five or six of these comrades, more or less involuntarily on both sides, at dinners which the Association for Friendship with Foreign Countries, our sponsoring escorts, insisted on giving in each city to welcome visiting "foreign friends" (the new official designation for all foreigners). In the presence of the local commissar as presiding host, subordinates hardly venture a word; conversational attempts are left to the guests through an interpreter. The commissar, genial but bored, confines himself to the toast-drinking routine and suavely avoids any conversation above the level of "How long have you been in China?" and "How long will you stay?" These men, at least those we met, do not convey an impression of quality above the union-boss level. They may be dedicated Maoists under the surface, or they may represent the inevitable formation of a new power group to replace the old, the very thing Mao is trying to avoid. As always the foreigner feels inadequate to penetrate the reality.

III

The Countryside

THE farmer is the eternal China. In the Sian Provincial Museum one can see a tomb carving of a Han Dynasty man driving a single-furrow iron plough pulled by a team of bullocks—and just outside town see the same arrangement functioning unchanged after two thousand years. In the fields groups of figures working together bend over the never-ending, back-breaking task of cultivation: transplanting rice seedlings, weeding the young corn, hoeing the vegetables, scything the ripe wheat or rice, and beginning over the plowing and harrowing of the field for the second crop.

In the north, plowing is by mule or bullock and occasionally, on the lands of a fortunate commune, by tractor. In the south and in the Yangtse Valley, the gray water buffalo with flat head and crescent horns that has not taken a hurried step for twenty centuries, provides the power. Here too, occasionally, a motored plough with a man walking between the handles can be seen lurching axle-deep through the mud of a wet paddy field, looking awkward and incongruous. Whatever the place and whatever the power, the bending human figures under straw hats are never absent from the scene.

Bent backs and straw hats are as integral to China as the gas station to America.

To the eye rural China is beautiful. Terraced slopes braced by strips of stone walls rise like earth ripples on the hills. The valleys below hold orchards and tile-roofed farmhouses and fields of wheat or corn or *kaoliang*, which looks like corn except that its grain is borne in a feathery cluster at the top. In the wide bed of a shallow river women and children scrub clothes against the rocks. Farther south, thatched roofs appear and yellow-flowered squash vines climb over them and over everything else, hiding the debris of farmyards. Fields of vegetables and rows of string-bean vines on neatly tied tripods make patterns against the flat rich green of rice paddies where the gleam of water shows through. Haystacks, some long, some conical, some with hat-brim tops looking peculiarly Chinese, fill the right places in the landscape as if an artist had placed them. Where there are canals, old wooden scows with dark sails move between the fields. In the distance mountains are never far away.

China has no landscape without figures. Through a lake of broad-leaved pink-flowering lotus, black-clad women with streaming hair wade waist-deep in water to pick the edible roots, making a picture so strange and poetic that they seem to belong to some ancient legend. On a village threshing floor chaff is shaken from the grain in shallow baskets; nearby a mule attached to a pole turns the millstone on his ceaseless round. A fishermen by a stream, looking exactly as he might in a Tang painting, tends a round-bottomed net hung from a bamboo frame. Where the stream flows by a village, three wizened old men retired from field work sit on a board turning a water wheel with their feet.

In the rice regions the early crop, already harvested, is spread out in neat golden bundles to dry. Alongside, after the soil has been turned and meticulously hoed and harrowed and the water pumped back, the thin, pale seedlings of the late crop, transplanted by hand, begin the cycle over again. Weeding, spraying, and fertilizing are still to come. No crop takes so much labor as the rice of Asia, but the yield per unit of land feeds the most mouths. The Chinese call wheat "the lazy man's crop."

The policy of dispersing industry to the countryside has already invaded the beauty. From the train window crossing the area between the Yellow River and the Yangtse, power line grids and the tall smokestacks and sharp outlines of factories suddenly appear here and there.

Old and new exist together. High on a hill in Shensi the fans of a radar station are visible. On the roadside below, a large grass-covered mound with a smoking chimney on top signifies a village brickmaking kiln. Boys and women with buckets dangling from shoulder poles carry night soil from a pit to spill on the fields, and elsewhere a group moves among the corn in a cloud of chemical spray. Insecticide is so important in today's China that in one ballet we saw in Peking the girl dancers appeared with handsprayers as part of their costume. Except for locusts, insects seem extraordinarily absent, and birds too in consequence. For the sake of agricultural yield, China has taken a long step toward silent spring. Chemical fertilizer is spread by hand from baskets, and in one beanfield we passed, by women doling it from wash basins with measuring spoons.

The rural reality is of course less idyllic than the view. The soft clay soil is dust in dry weather and clinging mud impossible to escape after a rain. In one small farm village near the Yellow River of perhaps twenty or thirty houses encircled by a crumbling clay wall, pigs, ducks, chickens, mules, donkeys, and people merged in the mud, and bullocks lay in it comfortably sleeping. What farm life must be like in the sodden snow of winter with temperatures below freezing is imaginable. Communes are slowly improving the housing but the backlog is vast: the rural population living in communities under 2,000 is estimated at 500,000,000 or approximately 100,000,000 households. Not all have been communalized. Some still cultivate tiny front-yard plots of corn or vegetables no more than ten or twelve feet square, although their land, we were told, is state-owned. A privy here was simply a hole in the ground with two flat stones placed on top in the form of a V.

Though painful in the making, communalized farming is by now the rule and the law. At a meeting of a Production Brigade (one unit of a commune) in Shensi, the team leaders, each representing some twenty to twenty-five households, were brown and wrinkled traditional peasants in work-soiled clothes, many of them older men, each with a towel turban wrapped around his head. Three of the team leaders were women. The Vice-Chairman of the Brigade's Revolutionary Committee was the type of village elder one would not have expected could read, but he spoke from notes written down in a pocket notebook. Each member in turn reported his team's progress in the second round of weeding, the second application of fertilizer, and the threshing of already harvested wheat. No. 5 Team was short of manpower and had to call on the old women and children for this task. Throughout the talk the importance given to chemical fertilizer was notable. More than Maoist thought, this is what has raised yield in China. The best time for the third application of insecticide, new to this village, was debated. Following the team leaders, an "educated youth" of about sixteen or seventeen, sent to the Brigade after graduation from Middle School for his three-year term of manual labor, spoke up to urge greater use of the "scientific" knowledge of the young. He was earnestly supported by the local schoolteacher.

The only obvious Government or Party man present, a gray-haired individual in glasses with a sophisticated face, was the Commune representative. Remaining silent throughout the discussion, he spoke only at the end to remind members to repair storehouse roofs against heavy rainfall, and to report a new method of shooting rockets in the air to disperse hail. Except for a glancing reference by the schoolteacher, not a single Maoist slogan or exhortation about the "struggle for production" or "in agriculture learn from Dachai," or "repudiate the Revisionists and capitalist-roaders" was mentioned, although doubtless this would not have been true of a younger group. It was the first, and except for a brilliant performance of traditional acrobats, magicians, and jugglers in Sian, the only such relief during the whole of our visit to China.

Mechanization of agriculture to replace the water buffaloes, the shoulder-pole baskets, and the bent human backs is the great goal. One could almost indulge in the dream that the Chinese might close themselves off from advancing history, as the last emperors tried vainly to do, and having got rid of the oppression of landlords and taxes and the cruelty of real want, might remain, despite the hard life, an agricultural people, both for the world's sake and their own. It somehow suits them.

IV

The Changed and Unchanging

THE two most striking physical features of China today are the new tree-planting and the old transportation by animal- and man-drawn cart.

Willows, sycamores, and countless varieties of poplars and cypress in multiple and flourishing rows, often under-planted with shrubs and hedges, supply shade and greenness in the city streets and extend for miles along the roads outside. Trees have been richly planted in parks, on campuses, factory grounds, new housing lots, airports, military barracks, dam sites, river banks. In the new part of Chengchow the avenues lined with double rows of sycamores already thirty feet high are spectacular. Nanking and Suchow have no street without shade. Nurseries of thin saplings can be seen everywhere. The "greening" campaign, as it is called, is said to have lowered the implacable summer heat in the baked cities of the north and the muggy cities of the Yangtse Valley by two degrees. In the hills it has begun to get a grip on the soil that had been allowed to erode and slide away in the rivers unchecked for centuries.

Afforestation is one of those civic works that was simply not undertaken in China before what is officially called "Liberation," that is, the Communist take-over in 1949. In Manchu times, local officials lived by the cut they could take out of tax-collecting and were disinclined to spend any of it on projects for the public welfare. After the Revolution of 1911, the "People's Welfare" was one of the Three Principles of the Kuomintang Party founded by Sun Yat-sen and inherited by Chiang Kai-shek, but it got lost in the difficulties of consolidating political power and of invasion by the Japanese. Until now the Yangtse was never bridged —not at Nanking although it was the national capital during 1929-49; nor upstream at the triple city of Wuhan where railroad cars on the main north-south line had to be carried over by ferry; nor farther up at Chungking, Chiang Kai-shek's war-time capital for eight years. Now bridges carry traffic across the river at all three places.

In Honan, province of the ghastly famine of 1942–43, a canal that took ten years to build has been cut through rock and mountain to carry water and electric power to stony Linhsien County whose people used to walk six miles to fetch water by bucket. Less spectacular but in the same spirit, a 400-man factory in Loyang has developed from twelve original workers and one sewing machine to make rubber-soled shoes for soldiers and peasants who once walked on straw.

How far China remains from its goal of modernization, however, lies under one's eyes every day in the endless procession of two-wheeled carts moving in and out of the provincial cities. This, not the trucks that serve Canton, Shanghai, and Peking, is the wider reality of China. Drawn by mixed teams or tandems of donkey, mule, and horse or by the straining muscles of a man between the shafts, with added pulling rope around a shoulder pad, the carts carry gravel, manure, bricks, building stone, sand, iron pipes, bottled drinks, earthenware jars, mountainous piles of scallions, red onions, melons, and other produce, roped loads of tires, boxes, chairs, waste paper and rags, bags of grain, bags of fertilizer, blocks of ice, baskets of coal, heavy tree trunks twenty feet long, and everything else the country sends to the city and vice versa.

Some, pulled by children, carry grandma sitting under an umbrella; some, pulled by grandma, carry children. Every animal-drawn cart carries, in addition to the driver, a second figure sprawled asleep on top of the load. Whole lives must be thus spent plodding along the roads, at such creeping pace when the load is heavy that once we drove past two haulers of scrap iron in the morning and on returning three hours later saw the same men only a few blocks farther on. Though some of the plodders are brawny young men, most are thin, muscular, workworn, soiled, and sweating toilers who may no longer have a landlord to oppress them but whose labor has not been much alleviated since the old days. A scrawny old woman bent against the weight of a load of wire rods bears little relation to the sturdy rosy ever-smiling maiden idyllically picking grapes who represents ideal proletarian womanhood on China's magazine covers. Often the heaviest loads are pulled by the oldest men as if (whisper it not in Mao's land of "struggle") the Marxist young, like any other, may have little inclination for the hardest work.

In the canal area, transportation is by barge, much of this too propelled by manpower. While some barges in long trains are pulled by tug on the Grand Canal, others are dragged by rope by plodders along the bank. On the smaller canals, single scows are moved by a man poling at snail's pace or bending his back to an oar pushed back and forth on a fulcrum at the stern.

How will all this human labor be used when and if China's transportation gradually becomes mechanized? The goal is so far from realization that it is hardly a worry, yet there are already signs that urban labor is underemployed. China's boasted record of full employment, which they like to tell you is the result of a planned economy as against the evils of our competitive private enterprise, is only achieved by assigning large numbers to more or less nominal jobs with no real function. Retinues of junior assistants follow every "leading cadre" like a claque, and a superabundance of personnel stands around in hotel corridors vaguely waiting for something to do. No fewer than six staff members of a "Friendship" store for foreigners clustered around the foreign exchange desk to supervise the cashing of one American Express check. At the Nanking Observatory nine staff members at one time were engaged in moving a bag of sand—which one could have handled—to mend a terrace. The cost of keeping people employed must be as great if not greater than our system of supporting the unemployed on welfare. The burden looms heavily over the future.

V

The Neighborhood Committee

Aᶠᵀᵉʳ transportation, housing is the most backward aspect of China. Although given to drastic street widening and bursts of Soviet gigantism in public squares and buildings, the authorities have preferred to let new housing adjoin new industry in the new sectors of provincial capitals rather than attempt urban renewal of the old inner city. The new housing, in the form of three- and four-story apartment buildings or brick cottage-type rows, is a tremendous improvement over the old but cannot begin to meet the need. Lining the old streets and extending behind them in a maze of alleys and courtyards are the clay cabins (they can hardly be called houses) of one or two dark rooms with dirt or stone floors that are home for millions of inhabitants. A community faucet or sometimes only a pump serves for running water. Electricity has been extended to most if not all, at least sufficient for a single bulb, but it never seems to be turned on until after absolute nightfall. Hankow exhibits a specialty of two-story wooden shacks so dilapidated that they lean wearily from the upright and with gaps between the boards look as if they must collapse tomorrow. So confined is space in all the old housing that the *kang* (or in the south movable beds), a small table, and one or two chairs, plus some sort of cooking arrangement and possibly a sewing machine placed next to the front door for light, suffice a family for furniture. Not unnaturally, at least in summer, the inhabitants tend to sit, eat, wash, tend babies, play cards and Chinese chess, hang up the laundry, and barber each other's hair on the sidewalk. In Hankow they bring out their beds and sleep in the street. Yet every day out of all this emerge streams of surprisingly neat, clean, and cheerful people (except in Canton where nobody is neat).

The new is at work here at the starting level in the Neighborhood Committee, the basic organ of the masses. Five or six of these local units make up a Street Committee, which is the lowest unit of state government. (Although the designations seem reversed, they are the Chinese usage.) Size varies according to the district; the Chao Chang Neighborhood Committee we visited in the old sector of Loyang represented 440 people in 80 households and belonged to a Street Committee of 1,800 people in 443 households. The Street Committee has its assigned Party member through whom government functions but the seven members of the Neighborhood Committee are "elected by the masses," that is, by their neighbors. Voting is by a show of hands, and the voters are the housewives and retired adults remaining at home, one or more per household. Here is the smallest cell of that share in control over their own fate so long denied to the common people of China. Here, too, of course, is where indoctrination begins.

The "old women" (meaning over forty) are clearly the power in the neighborhood. The three who met us were the type now frequently seen of exceedingly spruce, good-looking, simple women wearing spotless jackets of the side-closing old-fashioned kind and the silver wristwatches that are clearly a sign of status. (Under the proletarian puritanism imposed by the Cultural Revolution, watches also represent the last bit of glitter allowed.) With an official of the Street Committee carefully listening, the women described their Four Tasks. (Being a people who like life in a formal framework, the Chinese are only comfortable when they can arrange things in fixed numbers: the Three Principles, the Four Olds, the Eight Points, the Three Mountainous Burdens, and so on.)

First is the organization of study groups of "Marxism-Leninism and Mao Tse-tung Thought" among the older people which meet three times a week for four hours at a time. This seems like a lot of ML & M (in China one begins forcibly to abbreviate the slogans), but the women explained to us that "the masses have an urgent desire to learn." They said the enthusiasm resulting from these discussions of how to "serve the people" leads to "good deeds" among their neighbors: for instance, marketing for a woman overburdened at home; or establishing a free tea stand for carters entering the city when it was discovered that such people were very thirsty and knew no place to get a drink; or directing a bewildered visitor from the country to the local police register for help in locating his relatives. In the past these were people whose struggle for survival was so close to the edge as to allow no leeway for mutual assistance. Now they were taking part in the social process, and the pride with which they told these incidents was vibrant and very moving.

In the course of the study groups forty women of the neighborhood in the age group over forty had learned to read, to the extent of recognizing 100 characters.

The second task is "organizing the masses for production." Individuals are encouraged to seek jobs in factories and mines, small street factories are organized, for example, a forge or a one-room garment factory with a cutting table and six sewing machines, or a plant for assembling electric burners from factory-made parts (these were for export). Part-time production is also encouraged at home: for example, in the tiny courtyards of the homes we visited, the current project was assembling egg boxes by two or three women working together and paid at piece-work rates. What are called "commerical services," that is, a cook-shop, barber shop, cobbler's shop, or bicycle repair, come under the supervision of the Street Committee at prices fixed by the city.

The third task is to pass down to the masses the policies and instructions of the Government, and reflect back to the leadership the opinions of the masses. The fourth, under the title Social Welfare, consists mainly in educating the people in hygiene and sanitation, and conducting the permanent and high-pitched Love-the-Army campaign in the form of "Support the families of the PLA, Defenders of the Motherland." On August 1, which is Army Day, this was expressed by groups of children carrying the Red Flag to the doors of PLA families and singing songs of praise in the shrill raucous Chinese voice at ear-shattering volume.

Such is a microcosm of Communist society. It must be viewed in terms of a people who politically and materially are at a different stage of history than the Western democracies and whose needs are not our needs.

VI

The Mental Diet

As prescribed by Mao thirty years ago, cultural and intellectual exercise exists only to serve the Revolution. As such it becomes propaganda. Its foundations in China are firm, its structure protective. It exhorts, reassures, and has an answer for everything.

On the basis that Marxism is "irrefutable truth" and Mao Tse-tung Thought the one and only "correct revolutionary line," it presumes an ongoing struggle between "the two lines." The other line is Revisionism, meaning the effort to revert to the "Capitalist road" as represented by Liu Shao-chi, the veteran Communist and former President until his ouster in 1967, now the Anti-Christ of the system. This is the class struggle which is perpetual and never won because "bourgeois thinking" never gives up its effort to subvert the Revolution, and is never defeated (if it were, there would be no "struggle," which is essential to the system). Victory will only come with the final achievement of Socialism, which like the Kingdom of Heaven or the Second Coming lies always ahead.

Meanwhile, the main Maoist principles for keeping the struggle going are: 1) Serve the People; this

33

is the whole purpose of the society. 2) Increase production; all former "consumer" cities and communities must become producers and self-suppliers. 3) Self-reliance; the people down to the most local level must generate their own innovations and energies for the increase of production. 4) Continuing renewal of "revolutionary consciousness" and continuing guard against divorce from the reality of manual labor and the life of the masses. 5) Non-aggression and non-interference in the affairs of other states, based on the dictum that China can never be aggressive because aggression is incompatible with Socialism. (Non-interference is a rather more elastic matter.)

Sixth and most recent—and weakest—is the principle that all states are equal in status, Albania no less than Russia, Yemen on a par with the United States, and China is the friend of all based on a firm distinction, where necessary, between "good" peoples and "bad" governments. This convenient credo permits the new "friendship" with countries like the United States and Japan while maintaining an alert against the designs of imperialism and militarism, and at the same time reassures the Chinese people that all "peoples" are really on their side. If one suggests to them that under the Western system of representative government, the idea of a chasm between bad government and good people is a delusion and that in fact democratic governments, despite protest and opposition, tend on the whole to reflect their electorates, the Chinese remain happily unconvinced. They rest on Marxist dogma that the working-class "masses" are ipso facto always right and thus cannot support what is wrong, like the war in Vietnam. If one suggests that America has no working class conscious of identity as such, they do not comprehend.

The media for communicating these six principles and their basic premise make up in persistence what they lack in variety. The basic form is study groups of Marxism-Leninism and Mao Tse-tung Thought in school, neighborhood, office, commune, and factory. At the Steel Smelting Plant in Taiyuan employing 50,000 workers, the study groups meet after work for one and one-half hours four times a week with one session devoted to technical subjects and three to political thought and current affairs, occasionally varied by recreation and sport.

When it comes to reading matter, there are two national newspapers, *The People's Daily* and *The Workers' Daily*, distributed by mail subscription, plus various provincial papers. Content is more lectures than news and anything but fresh. On July 6, 1972, an editorial in *The People's Daily* (which it was thought worthwhile to reprint in *The Peking Review*, edited for foreigners) stated: "The extremely important instruction, 'Read and study seriously and have a good grasp of Marxism,' was issued by our great leader Chairman Mao after summing up the Party's experience in the struggles between the two lines. . . . Leading cadres of the Party committees have warmly responded to Chairman Mao's call and conscientiously studied the works of Marx, Engels, Lenin, and Stalin and Chairman Mao's works. This is becoming common practice and has brought certain results."

There are two glossy magazines published in many languages and intended mainly for foreigners though eagerly read by the Chinese, and at least one popular magazine presumably obtained, like the newspapers, by mail, for there are no newsstands except for occasional small street tables displaying a newspaper and a few pamphlets and Mao Thought booklets. To imagine an American or European city without its newsstands in streets, stores, and subways is to visualize how striking is their lack in China. Wall newspapers mounted behind glass exist, some with newsprint, most given over mainly to photographs exhibiting various proletarian triumphs in harvesting, athletics, shipbuilding, barefoot-doctoring, and other examples of "overfulfilling the quota."

Although television exists to the extent of one or two hours of programming a day, I never saw a set outside the hotels for foreigners nor was ever shown one in factory, commune, school, street committee, or other institution, much less a home. Radios, however, are prized: of the eighty households in the Chao Chang neighborhood in Loyang, twenty-two possessed radios, and young men walk in the parks carrying transistors.

Bookstores, including foreign language bookstores, are almost as much a shock as the missing newsstands, for instead of color and variety they display pile upon pile of little monotone booklets either of Marxist classics (judging by the remainder piles even loyal Chinese are not avidly interested in *The Critique of the Gotha Programme*, which is understandable) or Maoist Thought or illustrated storybooks based on the film of the opera of the ballet of *The White-Haired Girl* (which has been playing for twenty years) or *The Red Detachment of Women* or *Dragon River* or another of the familiar dramas whose theme is invariably the heroic collective triumph over landlords, Japanese, counter-revolutionaries, and other evils.

That this fare needs some enrichment has evidently been recognized by the authorities, for new editions (with suitable introductions) of the classic Chinese novels—*Water Margins, Three Kingdoms,* and others—have appeared, as well as the works of some "bourgeois" Western economists. When these went on sale, the crush at the bookstores, according to foreign residents of Peking, was epic, and copies are now hard to come by as they are always sold out.

To instill self-confidence, triumph is the dominant note in all forms of communication, especially in the permanent outdoor posters set up in public squares and in front of public buildings. The raised proletarian fist, the outthrust chest, the heroic gaze into the far horizon combine to express invincible determination by figures resembling overfed Paul

Bunyans, usually wearing fur caps with ear flaps left carelessly open to the winter wind. The same heroic note dominates music broadcast over the loudspeakers. Generally in the Western mode, since Chinese music despite its decibel count is too un-inflected to express triumph, this form of exhortation reaches a climax every few bars like a parade for-ever passing by but never ending. The same themes and songs are learned from kindergarten up in song-and-dance programs. Excerpts from the famous ballets and self-composed dance-dramas are per-formed by the schoolchildren with poise, gusto, frightening proficiency, and such fixed smiles of happiness as would make an American chorus line by comparison look melancholy. Amateur groups and propaganda teams carry these song-and-dance programs around the country; like early America, China still relies heavily on self-entertainment.

Art too serves the class struggle. "Following Chairman Mao's teaching," reports the official news agency Hsinhua on a recent exhibition of People's Art, "the painters take as their main theme the emancipation of the poor and lower middle peasants from heavy exploitation by the landlord class. Every stroke bears out ardent love for socialism and im-placable hatred for feudalism and capitalism." A stone carving, "Ode to the Plum Blossom," reports *The Peking Review,* "describes the dauntless in-tegrity of proletarian revolutionaries."

On this diet China's people under thirty-five are left strikingly uninformed. They know nothing

about anything outside their immediate job or beyond their own neighborhood. They ask no questions, have no curiosity and do not speculate.
When we were informed that famed Hangchow,
normally on every visitor's schedule, was suddenly
"closed to foreigners," and our guide could give us
no reason, my daughter, after futile questioning, at
last expostulated, "Well, what do you *imagine* is
the reason?" "It is not practical to imagine," he
replied.

They know nothing whatever about the past prior
to "Liberation" in 1949. The past is one great big
black landlord planted upon a foundation of feudalism which was gradually transformed into foreign-
aggressive-imperial-colonialism still upholding the
landlord. All history, prehistory, and yesterday are
covered under this one rubric. It is all the Chinese
know about their own history, much less any other.
All historic time prior to 1949 is a blur. Apropos of
some distinctly eighteenth-century frescoes on a
temple wall, the local guide informed us these
were "pre-Liberation." The Opium Wars of 1840–
60, the Boxer Rebellion of 1900, and the Japanese
War of the 1930s and '40s are barely seen as distinct in date, and the Chinese are virtually unaware
that anyone fought the Japanese but themselves—
themselves being confined to the Communist 8th
Route Army. When I asked a high school history
class if they knew how the Japanese were eventually defeated, one girl replied, "By the 8th Route
Army and the Soviet Red Army." When I asked if

they knew anything about the American role in the war, the same girl said, after a prolonged and general silence, that she had heard of what came through in translation as "Pearl Port," suggesting that our interpreter too was unfamiliar with the name and with America's four-year effort that followed.

Chinese Communism itself appears as solely the work of Mao and the 8th Route Army with an assist from Stalin. No Chinese other than Mao is ever pictured in the public propaganda. He shares history only with Marx, Engels, Lenin, and Stalin whose portraits in a row of four huge pictures one sees at every turn. No matter how often one sees it, the glorification in China of these thoroughly European faces, especially the last, remains embarrassing.

So numbing is the monotony and so simplistic the content of all this that it is a puzzle how the Chinese can bear it. The puzzle, however, has an answer: in the first place the relevant people of China today are the masses who, as Mao himself rather condescendingly put it, were "blank." He added, "And on blank pages the most beautiful words can be written." So can the most banal or the most anything, for people who start from blank will absorb whatever they are given; they have no criteria by which to judge and have not yet developed the capacity to be bored.

Secondly, the Chinese have traditionally been accustomed to living within a prescribed pattern of behavior. Confucianism was just that; it too had its slogans inscribed on public walls and prescriptions that survive in the English byword, "Confucius says . . ." Chiang Kai-shek used the same style (with no success) in his New Life movement, "Do not spit. Correct your posture. Kill rats and flies." In that sense Mao Tse-tung Thought follows an old form.

Finally, if content is considered in terms of the needs of the people and the dynamics of the Communist program rather than in terms of what an educated Western mind requires for nourishment, it is apparent that Mao's prescriptions make a good deal of sense—certainly more than "I am Gigi; fly me to Miami," or "The toothpaste with sex appeal," or other adages of our society. The difference is, of course, that in China the slogans are meant and taken seriously.

One can see them in action. At a railroad crossing a PLA soldier on guard at the place actually stepped down into the road to help a peasant get his heavily loaded cart into motion again after the train had passed. He was "serving the people," a thing that could never have happened in the old days when the soldier was both scum and the people's bane. At a staff meeting of a small 24-hour grocery store in Shanghai the question at issue was whether to put a bicycle pump in service during the night shift when the bicycle repair shop across the street was closed. Since no charge could be made for the service, the pump would represent added cost and time for the store. But the staff had been affected the night before by a worker with a flat tire whom they had to send away unaided, knowing he would have to walk the rest of the way and be late for his job at the factory. To support "increased production," the staff agreed it was their duty to maintain a bicycle pump.

This is Communist China in practice. China-watchers on the outside who take its pulse-beat through its words and published statements will never record the reality because the words, taken alone, are irritating if not fatuous. It is only when one sees them acted out in the lives of the people that an understanding of today's China is possible.

Nevertheless, the assumption of infallibility, the twisting of the record, the suppression of fact are creating an uninformed and misinformed—although a motivated—public. One would like to believe that knowledge must break through, that truth conquers, that no people can be kept in obedient consensus for long, but I am not sure of these propositions regarding China. Nine-tenths of the mainland population may be so thoroughly and contentedly indoctrinated that it will be long before they are open to new ideas.

VII

Preserving the Heritage

WESTERN visitors often arrive in China wondering whether Communism has destroyed the heritage of ancient treasures or left them to the ruin of neglect. As it turns out, a Department for the Preservation of Historic Relics has been functioning since 1949, and under its supervision palaces, pagodas, temples, and gardens are in better condition, in most cases, than at any time since their original occupants departed. The Communists are uncovering, repairing, restoring, and opening all monuments to the public with the stated purpose, of course, of exhibiting how the propertied class exploited the labor of the people for their private luxury. Simultaneously if somewhat disjointedly, the object is to show how China's famed heritage of arts is owed to "the wisdom of the masses" because theirs was the labor that built a Ming tomb or fired the glaze on porcelain or embroidered an emperor's silk coat. The share of the original architect, artist, or designer goes unmentioned, leaving the public to conclude that the conception sprang full-blown from the brow of the masses.

This is the obvious rationale necessary to justify

the investment of effort on relics of the leisure class. But after visiting museums and reconstructed sites of all kinds from Neolithic villages to the last home of Dr. Sun Yat-sen in Shanghai, I could not escape the feeling—which I must stress is only my own impression—that the work of preservation and archeological discovery is being done for its own sake, partly to keep a lot of people busy but also out of a kind of subdued pride in the national heritage.

Since such pride comes perilously close to "non-proletarian thinking," it cannot be openly expressed under the stern purity of purpose prevailing since the Cultural Revolution. Works of art are not accorded any aesthetic value per se but only the propaganda value of their subject matter. The result is an extraordinary disinterest in the aesthetic. Of the fifty or more guides, escorts, and local site guides we encountered on our way—they were always supplied in multiples—I cannot remember one expressing appreciation of any object, even the scenery, for its beauty. Beauty for its own sake, like sex, is officially out of favor.

Archeology, which does not require ideas, is the biggest cultural activity in China. It was given sudden stimulus by the wave of engineering projects carried out by the Communists which, in digging foundations for canals, dams, and factories, turned up hundreds of tombs and old inhabited sites never investigated before. An extraordinary wealth of artifacts has been found, many in perfect condition, some unique, others of a type previously unseen and invaluable. The most excitement was caused by the Jade Emperor, actually a burial covering of square-cut pieces of jade sewn together like a medieval coat of mail. The most exquisite is the Lady with a Lamp, a gilded bronze statuette of a gently kneeling figure.

The cream of the finds, including these two, was on exhibit this summer in Peking. Others have been spread through the provinces, with special effect in the museums of Sian, Loyang, and Nanking and in the reconstructed Neolithic village at Sian. Artifacts and figures are labeled by dynasty and also by sociological system, that is, "Slave society" for the Chou Dynasty, 1122–249 B.C., "Feudal society" beginning with the Han, 206 B.C. to A.D. 220, and so on. The delicate question of class origins has been settled by the finding from late Neolithic times of skeletons buried nakedly without pots or jars, indicating the first slaves as distinct from slave-owners. Besides being ideologically malleable, archeology is collective in effort and marvelously suited to the Marxist state.

Preservation of palaces and temples finds its natural justification in public use. All the famed sites are now public parks, well cared for and heavily used, often with outdoor cafes or refreshment stands under ancient pines. The Imperial City in Peking, with its halls of audience and residence and courtyards and marble ramps, is now as crowded as New York's Metropolitan Museum, unlike my last visit in 1935 when the buildings were closed and the grounds eerily empty with weeds growing in the courtyards. The Summer Palace outside the city with its terraced pavilions and gardens and lake for boating is no less crowded and infinitely cleaner and safer than Central Park. Here and in many other parks, gardening is first class, with lotus ponds, peony beds, rose bushes, potted oleander and other flowering shrubs, and all the familiar annuals. In every city—at least judging by the eleven we visited—new parks have been added, like the Working People's Park in Loyang, also called, somewhat inconsistently, Wang Tsen or Imperial Park because it was the site of the Chou Dynasty capital. The peony beds here are of such remarkable size and magnificence that to see them in bloom in April would probably be worth the 10,000-mile voyage.

In Peking most of the buildings of the Imperial City, including the last Empress's bedroom, are open, with furniture and decor restored as they were when last occupied. There are no guards, at least none recognizable in uniform. In the treasure room, the fantastic objects of jade, gold, ivory, and jewels are housed in glass cases but otherwise unprotected. What is left of the national collection of porcelains and paintings, after the major share was taken off to Taiwan by Chiang Kai-shek, is for some reason not on public view and only to be seen by special request. The supreme painting of old China is one form of art which cannot by any stretch of the dialectic be represented as a product of the masses and is therefore very little exhibited, if at all.

Since religion has suffered the shutdown common under Communist regimes, many Buddhist and Taoist temples listed in guidebooks are not to be seen, perhaps because of vandalism suffered during the ravages of the Cultural Revolution or perhaps because they are simply closed. Others of special renown, like the Temple of the Five Hundred Disciples at Suchow with its 500 glowing golden statues, or the rich buildings and grounds of the former Jen Ci monastery in Shansi, or the Lung Men caves of Buddhist sculptures, have been preserved for public visiting without, as far as we could see, any anti-religious propaganda attached.

The propaganda varies erratically in stress. It is all but invisible at the classical gardens of Suchow, although they represent the acme of leisured existence where rich mandarins retired to live in highly contrived Marie Antoinette–type rusticity. One by one, with great expenditure of labor which China can easily spare, these are being minutely replanted, polished, and restored, perhaps for their tourist value, although how they escaped the Red Guards at the height of their frenzy is a mystery. On the other hand, propaganda is heavy at the Ming Tombs, now excavated and publicly exhibited for the first time. Graphic charts claim to show that 30,000 men a day worked for six years, or 65,000,000 man-days, to build a useless tomb while every peasant household in the area was forced to contribute an average of 6.5 workers to the task.

Here, as in most museums, painted and modelled reconstructions portray peasant uprisings over the centuries with fierce spears and raised fists but little progress against feudalism. The accompanying texts, which I could not read, no doubt supplied convincing Marxist reasons why feudalism remained so long embedded in China. The object everywhere was to remind the viewer of the cruelty and oppression of the past as compared to the "liberation" of 1949.

One curious exception was in the realm of science. Alongside models in the Sian Museum of the first seismograph, astrolabe, and compass, and of the first man to use the pulse for medical diagnosis, the curators have displayed finely executed but imaginary portraits of the developers of these instruments and methods. The portraits clearly show men of the upper class with scholars' gowns and intellectual faces. Apparently the wisdom, in their case, is allowed to be their own without inspiration from the masses. What this aberration signifies, if anything, I do not know; perhaps only the comforting thought that Communism has its inconsistencies no less than Democracy.

VIII

Keeping the Revolution Green

I F Mao's place in history depended solely on his
leadership of China's belated revolution—in
which he had many associates now lost in the
shadows of Mao-worship—that place would be great
but not unique. His truly original contribution has
been his concept of ongoing revolution, his recognition that achievement of power is not the end,
but on the contrary the peril, because success
solidifies. Thus every revolution ends in a new
ruling class and every ruling class, by gripping the
status quo, ends in Revisionism, the final sin. It is
not the state that withers away but Revolution,
and with it the goal of Socialism.

To recognize this principle is open to anyone
with a sense of history, but Mao is probably the
first chief of state to act upon it to uproot and dis-
member his own power structure in order to restart
the revolution and keep it moving toward its goals.

This was the purpose and meaning of that
mysterious frenzy—as it came through to the West
in bewildering flashes—which swept China in 1966–
69 and is now sanctified as the great Proletarian
Cultural Revolution. Deliberately set in motion by
Mao and at least some like-thinking colleagues, it

was an act of extraordinary risk that could have wrecked the system. It activated the fanaticism of youth, which can be activated to anything, and set it rampaging through society, beating, persecuting, shaming, and leaving a wake of violence, ruin, and suicides. In the course of purging Liu Shao-chi and breaking up the settled bureaucracy which he supposedly headed, the movement also ignited a dangerous opposition of the Ultra Left whose object, more or less, was to shatter the whole establishment and achieve Socialism through anarchy. Factions arose and fought with spears and stones when they could not get arms. Only because the Army remained loyal as the arm of the Party was Mao able to apply the brakes, regain control, and begin to reconstruct his Government.

At present the domestic surface is calm; the vicious turmoil of only a few years ago seems to have left the public curiously unaffected. Their equanimity reminds one of a tantalizing remark by an English missionary named George Tradescant Lay who wrote in 1841, "The Government of China is purposely absurd but the people are reasonable in their views and conceptions."

To judge either the degree of damage wrought by the Cultural Revolution or the degree of renewed revolutionary impetus is not possible for a superficial visitor, but some of the cost is obvious. Although most of the purged bureaucracy below the top are said to have returned to their jobs after "re-education," the government has undoubtedly been weakened, both within the central

"Leading cadres" at a May 7th
Cadre School in Shensi

Pumping station for irrigation and
flood control at Yellow River

Author at the factory home of Mrs. Chang Si-lan

Transportation by cart

The family survives: grandparents and children in Loyang

Rural China:
Silo and grinding stone
Washday in Yenan

Loudspeaker on roof of a commune in Shensi

Women of the Neighborhood Committee in Loyang

Propaganda in the museums depicting
early peasant uprisings

Restoration work on Buddhist statues
in the Lung Men caves

Primary schoolchildren rehearsing
a dance with rifles in Nanking

Staring at foreigners

Politburo and in its authority over the provinces. The Ultra Left, angered by the return of the bureaucrats, is far from dead, and power struggles within the Party and Politburo apparently continue.

At the same time it is plain that the ideas of the Cultural Revolution have officially prevailed, at least in general lip service. "Reliance on the masses" is the password, and the painful process of "Struggle, Criticism, and Transformation," which refits a Revisionist or other erroneous thinker for service to the people, must still be endured. Struggle, Criticism, and Transformation —which emerges as SCAT in my abbreviation—is a great invention. For purposes of rehabilitation, it means repudiation of "Liu Shao-chiist crimes" followed by a change of heart through self-criticism, but it can also be used to cover up any situation in which Maoist control is not fully re-established or intramural struggle continues.

When I asked to meet members of a Writers' Union, if any, I was told there were "no writers in Peking," and the same was said of Shanghai, because they were all away in May 7th camps undergoing Struggle, Criticism, and Transformation. When I asked why Szechwan was "closed to foreigners," I was told the province was undergoing SCAT. The same explanation was offered for not taking me to visit the great Peking Public Library. In fact the whole library system must have been suffering a severe case of SCAT, for though I kept up the pressure, municipal libraries elsewhere remained off limits.

The campaign against Revisionism remains fierce. While Stalin's purges killed men, in China it is the idea which must be destroyed, must be dragged out, exposed, trampled, and stamped out. This requires unrelenting denunciation which the people repeat as dutifully as a congregation chanting responses to the minister. Every negative result in the past is explained as caused by the influence of Liu Shao-chi, and equally any current negative development—a poor harvest, an outbreak of disease, a foreign threat, or the persistence of dissenters escaping to Hong Kong—is the undercover work of "Liu Shao-chiist swindlers and criminals" who are somehow able to sway the true-thinking masses toward wrongdoing. Even the excesses of the Red Guards during the Cultural Revolution are laid to Revisionist infiltrators who instigated them to violence. The people are being educated in a conspiracy theory of evil, the easiest thing of all to believe in. It leaves Party and leaders unresponsible for error or failure.

The effect of the Cultural Revolution is crystallized in the universities. Because the sons and daughters of the ruling group were filling the classes, it was here that elitism was believed most dangerously developing, and as everyone knows the universities were actually closed down for two or more years.

Under tall trees on the old campus of Peking—or Peita—University, founded in 1898, we were told that only three or four of the faculty had been permanently eliminated as counter-revolutionaries because these individuals had refused to admit to "crimes" and therefore could not make a new start. One member of the English department, it was said, had even admitted to being a Kuomintang agent but after Struggle, Criticism, and Transformation, had been allowed to resume teaching. The distinguished professor of history and a younger associate with whom we talked told us that they themselves had been "repudiated by the students and masses." It had taken them a long time to admit the justice of the accusations but they finally came to recognize their errors and were now fully functioning again.

Listening to such talk from mature men, I was too embarrassed to look them in the eye. Outside, during the lunch hour, a loud speaker screamed the usual heroic music at a pitch that penetrated the entire area of what was supposed to be a place of learning.

Since 1970 the re-opened universities have been recruiting and enrolling only students from the masses, that is, from the ranks of workers, peasants, and soldiers. The new policy presumes that working-class experience of actual jobs in various fields fits these young men and women to make better use of an education for purposes of serving the revolution. If they have graduated from Junior Middle School, which finishes at about age sixteen, and have held a job for a few years, they are admitted on the recommendation of their work unit without any qualifying examination.

Of five boys I questioned in a dormitory room

at the Sian College of Engineering, one had been out of school eight years before coming to the university, one for six years, two for five years, and one for three years. They were eager, bright-eyed, very appealing youngsters but hardly equipped for higher education in the academic sense. Nor did they need to be. Courses are now virtually vocational. In the humanities the vocation is revolution: a student of history, for example, is taught in terms of social problems relating to the life of the masses and can look forward, we were told, to a career as a propagandist in which he can "serve the people of China and the world." In science, judging by the curriculum at Sian, the training is purely technical and mechanical.

Enrollment on the new basis is so far very limited: Peita with a normal capacity of 10,000 and a faculty of 2,100, admitted 1,000 students drawn from the whole country in 1972. Sian, with a capacity of 7,500 and a faculty and staff of 2,000, has a total student population this year of 1,400. Throughout the country the total number of university students now enrolled is estimated by professional China-watchers in Hong Kong at less than half a million. Grades have been abolished as a bourgeois device to exclude the masses.*

"Tragically unqualified," murmured a Harvard professor on his way out of China after visiting Peita. But the question is, qualified for what? The government of China has apparently made up its

* Grades and examinations have been restored since this was written.

mind, for the present, that it wants revolutionary impetus more than it wants advanced education; or perhaps that it fears elitism more than it needs intellectuals. China does not need to advance, it needs to catch up, and it may have decided that properly motivated technicians serve this purpose best.

Here, too, the risk is great. Meanwhile at the top, successive purges have left a vacuum below the aged veterans of the formative years: Mao, Chou En-lai, and Marshal Yeh Chien-ying, aged seventy, who is now filling the place of Lin Piao. The succession is undecided, the factions still at odds, and the threat of Soviet attacks looms over the border. Fear of invasion or nuclear attack preoccupies Peking and explains the obsessive emphasis on arms in the domestic propaganda.

Under such pressures from inside and out, can the Revolution be kept green, especially after the old guard goes? Under new men, will the insistent nature of a ruling class assert itself in China as anywhere else? Will Liu Shao-chiism revive without Liu Shao-chi? These questions hardly seem to concern the public; they do not ask; they seem to have faith. It has been said by a shrewd observer that they have taken their revolution more seriously than the Russians.

In quest of a more informed judgment than my own, I asked a foreign diplomat with long experience of China if he felt he was dealing in Peking with a stable government in control of the situation. "In control, yes; stable, no," he replied. "The storms that shake the system are part of it."

IX

Friendship with
Foreign Devils

ALTHOUGH the term "foreign devils" is no longer used in contemporary China—is in fact so obsolete that Chinese whom we met professed not to recognize or understand the phrase—the concept is alive and still governs, it seems to me, the Chinese attitude. China's present program, deriving from fear of Russia, is a determined campaign to cultivate the "friendship" of foreign peoples, but the treatment of foreigners is such a hothouse affair as to suggest that the Chinese are not at all at ease in the contact. Underneath, one suspects, the old view of foreigners as strange, unnatural, essentially unwanted creatures, part barbarian, part devil, has not changed fundamentally. The relationship is now conducted according to Marxist dogma but its underlying attitude is as much traditionally Chinese as Communist.

Two hundred years ago China's imperial rulers, secluded within their walls of conscious superiority, sensed a threat to a past-oriented society in the dynamism of the West, and tried with guile, persistence, and feeble force to limit contact and frustrate foreign entry. Today despite continuous incantation of the word "friendship," which we must have heard a hundred times a day throughout a forty-day visit, one cannot escape the impression that if only it were not for world pressures, Maoist China like that of the Ming and the Manchus would be happier if it could withdraw into the broad isolation of the Middle Kingdom.

Peking's present rulers, however, are perforce more realistic than the emperors; they know the world is too much with them, too pressing, and too close, to fend off or ignore or do without. They have already taken the great step of embracing a Western ideology in the form of Marxism-Leninism; there is no retreat now from the world. Their initial isolation, resulting from angry rejection of the West and failure to galvanize a revolutionary following in Asia, suddenly became dangerous after their break with Russia in the early 1960s. When the break developed into open hostility, the need for friends, or at least for new options and new alignments, became a necessity, however awkward ideologically. Hence Ping-Pong diplomacy, rapprochement first with the United States, then Japan, and fervent patronage of the small third-world nations.

Toward Westerners the approach is a curious mixture of exaggerated privilege and strict control. The privileges tend to become embarrassing especially in an otherwise egalitarian society. While the Chinese do not own private cars, the visitor always has a car at his disposal, not only for the planned program but for whatever purpose at whatever hour: at 6 A.M. if one wants to go out early to watch the waking city, at 10 P.M. to come home from the ballet, or for a private visit or shopping tour that might last several hours. The driver waits like an old-fashioned private chauffeur. His convenience is no more consulted, his working hours no more limited than if he were employed by John D. Rockefeller, Sr., in 1920. These arrangements are made by one's assigned escort who along with an interpreter is constantly in attendance.

Foreigners feel themselves surrounded by the trappings of an elite. They stay in separate hotels, dine in separate dining rooms—or screened off from the Chinese if there is only one dining room —travel in separate compartments on trains, wait in separate waiting rooms at the station, are cared for on a separate floor of the hospital. During intermission at the theater we are not left to stand among the crowd but are firmly guided to sit among other foreigners in a private reception room. On the lake at the Summer Palace we can not engage a rowboat to row ourselves like the Chinese but are grandly deposited in a large covered boat provided with tea and tablecloth and poled by two boatmen. In museums our guides push aside Chinese visitors from the exhibit cases to give us unnecessary room; on the bridge at Wuhan traffic is stopped so that we may cross over to view the river from the other side; at a park our car drives through a pedestrian entrance where the Chinese walk; at a railroad station after imperious horn-blowing we drive through a special gate right up to the tracks. At one of Chairman Mao's former residences in Yenan (all four of which are visited like stages of the Sacred Way in Jerusalem), a group of about fifty students, seated on the ground before an outdoor plaque listening to a lecture, rises on command to move out of our way as we approach.

Segregation, self-administered, is a feature in China, and one is sometimes uncertain, as in the screened dining rooms, who is Jim Crow, we or they. (Blacks from Africa are, of course, treated like any other foreigner.) The Chinese consider it a mark of preferment for a foreigner to eat apart, but one feels they also prefer it for themselves. In Yenan where a large new hotel was under construction and we asked what future use was planned for the present one, the reply was, "Oh, that will be for internal visitors."

Overseas Chinese who are now visiting the mainland in large numbers are treated as another distinct category between native and foreigner. Although China maintains the theory, like Israel, that its diaspora, regardless of citizenship, has the right of return, it treats the visiting racial compatriots brusquely. With the exception of some distinguished individuals, they are confined to separate hotels, travel under separate arrangements, and are kept as far as possible from mingling

with Westerners. When we made the acquaintance
of some overseas Chinese from New York and invited them to join us in the private reception room
at an evening performance, our escorts did not
trouble to conceal their disapproval. The motive
in all this obviously has to do with control and
surveillance since the overseas groups can be in-
filtrated by Kuomintang agents, but their treatment is also quite clearly second-class. Judging by
these various distinctions and pockets of apartheid
in Communist practice, it is plain that despite
ideology, the new Chinese, like the old, are not
great believers in the equality of humankind.

The odd thing is that having demolished extra-
territoriality and the unequal treaties, and every
last vestige of foreign penetration, and having de-
nounced and metaphorically trampled upon Westerners as imperialist criminals, reactionary oppressors, running dogs, paper tigers, and every
other variety of evil, the Chinese seem unable to
treat us in the flesh in any other way than as the
privileged characters of the bad old Treaty Port
days. Queried on this phenomenon, they reply that
the former treatment was exacted *from* them but
the present privileges are bestowed *by* them vol-
untarily from a desire to make their foreign friends
feel comfortable and enjoy their sojourn in China
under agreeable conditions.

This has validity up to a point and one is glad
enough to take advantage of it and not to have to

travel in the heat of summer in a crowded second-class compartment or eat in the public room of a restaurant surrounded by tables of staring men in their undershirts. The Chinese have an acute and very practical awareness of this problem and since their object is to make the foreigner feel well-disposed, they set about it by attention to his physical comfort, not by democratic leveling. They are probably justified by results although I think the cosseting is overdone.

My particular experience makes it ungracious to carp. I discovered on arrival that, as a guest of the Association for Friendship with Foreign Countries, I was a guest in every sense, including financial, and no amount of protests, pleas, and arguments about the awkward position it put me in as a journalist had the slightest modifying effect. A bureaucratic decision once taken is not easily changed in China. My category was "friend of the Chinese people" and, while cordial, this too was bothersome. I wrote the book that presumably earned it neither as friend nor un-friend but as a historian, which presupposes—if it does not sound pretentious to say so—a certain purity of intent. To the Chinese as Communists, a historian is a propagandist like every other servant of the state, so it would have been useless to try to explain my reservations.

A "friend of the Chinese people" is decidedly pampered. We had front-row seats—sometimes upholstered armchairs—reserved for us at evening dance performances arranged in the hotels; audiences rose and clapped on our arrival and departure; a special one-car train was put on to take us from Loyang to Chengchow out of schedule; a former cargo boat, cleaned up for passengers and supplied with tea table and twelve in crew, was summoned to give us alone an hour's cruise on the Yellow River. In Suchow, admittedly a town of rather special flavor, we were ensconced in a separate annex of the hotel with two suites, a private dining room, an attendant butler (there is no other word for him), and, besides the usual tea thermos, cigarettes, and fruit in the bedroom, a fresh plate of candies every day and a fresh arrangement of jasmine buds in the form of a brooch. With everything provided, I, like Queen Victoria, never held a railroad ticket or used a coin.

Yet the effect of all this gracious attention was not so much to make one feel oneself an object of friendship as of manipulation. And it was reminiscent. I looked up in *Stilwell* and read aloud to my daughter my own account of Wendell Willkie's visit to Chungking in 1943. "In the manipulation of foreigners every Chinese from amah and houseboy to the Generalissimo and Madame considered himself expert. In this matter Chinese confidence in themselves was supreme and their skills unsurpassed. They were adept, unrelenting, smooth and more often than not successful. . . . Willkie's visit supremely illustrated the Chinese process of influencing American public opinion. 'He's to be smothered,' Stilwell wrote. There was to be an unbroken schedule of banquets, receptions, reviews, dinners, visits to schools, factories, girl scouts, arsenals. He was to be installed in a Chinese guest house as the guest of the Chinese Government . . ."

Friendship of a kind that cannot easily be reversed tomorrow must have its roots in common interests and shared beliefs, and even between nations, in some personal feeling. Intercourse with Chinese is anything but personal. They never talk about their personal lives; they never bring wives to a banquet to meet foreigners, which makes the banquet clearly not a social occasion but a job, and no amount of routine toasts to "Friendship" can make it otherwise, especially as the Chinese Communists are neither so glib nor so practiced in the job as were the cohorts of Chiang Kai-shek. Even artificial friendship, however, is a step forward from hostility.

For domestic consumption the stress on "friendship" is essential. The theory is that capitalist governments are bad but people, that is the "masses," are good; therefore all peoples are friends of China and vice versa. This takes care of any incompatibility that a member of the Chinese public might feel between official denunciation of American imperialism on the one hand and personal welcome to individual Americans on the other, or between watching the former Japanese invaders depicted nightly on stage as atrocious villains while the Shanghai Ballet troupe tours Japan with fanfares of mutual friendship.

The doctrine is apparently found convincing by the public. One certainly meets a fund of genuine friendliness in the provincial cities and countryside expressed in smiles and spontaneous clapping. This new practice, derived perhaps from the Russians, has spread down to tiny children in rural villages who see a foreigner and clap of their own accord, which must say something of the attitude of their parents. Adults, too, in some places will clap on their own initiative. But during institutional visits the effect on the foreigner of being met coming and going by large groups rising to their feet and clapping is absolutely unnerving.

The other reaction to foreigners is staring. One cannot walk down a street or in a park, museum, store, or any public place without attracting crowds who fill the sidewalk or form a circle or just stop short and stare, openly, brazenly, greedily. Sometimes it is with frank curiosity, sometimes with utter astonishment as if we were Martians wearing feathers, or indeed foreign "devils." Given the continued propaganda that presents all foreigners in Chinese history as unrelieved oppressors and robbers, it is hardly surprising that the sudden appearance of foreign "friends" in Chinese streets causes mouths to drop open. Occasionally the stares express antagonism and remind one uneasily of the recent anti-foreign violence of the Cultural

Revolution and earlier outbursts of xenophobia over the last hundred years. Although our guides once or twice seemed unnecessarily nervous, we never once encountered outright hostility. The overwhelming impression was one of a naturally friendly people.

Once, as we were leaving a high school in Peking, a group of students crowded around us with intense eagerness at the door, each one trying to shake our hands as if it were terribly important to make physical contact, and all the faces glowing with real personal smiles (not the fixed ones of the dance performances). One felt an outpouring almost of love which was hard to fathom. Perhaps they were trying to demonstrate their faith in the good people–bad government doctrine.

Whether official China counts seriously on disengaging peoples from their governments I cannot say. But motives for the friendship campaign are certainly not sentimental, as I learned from the most illuminating remark made to me in China. It came in conversation at Peking University with the President (in current terms, Vice-Chairman of the University's Revolutionary Committee) Chou P'ei-yuan and Professor of History Chou I-liang. In the course of discussing the startling shifts in the foreign policy of both our countries as reflected in the recent rapprochement, I asked whether the decision to open relations with an imperialist-aggressor super-power caused much disruption or dissent in the Central Committee. Not at all, I was blandly told; negotiating with an antagonist was consistent with Chinese Communist practice; they had negotiated, even collaborated in the past with Chiang Kai-shek, why not Nixon? This I understood, I replied, but was it part of negotiating with an antagonist to warmly welcome his nationals as "friends"? This time something more than the ritual answer came through. "Friendship," said Professor Chou I-liang with a slight bow in our direction, "is a form of struggle, too."

Struggle is the key word in Communist China. Nothing is casual, nothing—including contact with foreigners—left to find its own level. Like the Emperors and the Kuomintang, the Communists consider the contact something to be managed for a purpose. They are very concerned with making a good impression and believe that by controlling what the visitor sees and what he does not see that they can control, or at any rate condition, his reaction. All tours are programmed and escorted, usually by a plethora of personnel caused by the addition of local escorts in each city and local guides at each site. All conversations, meetings, and briefings must be conducted through an interpreter whether or not there is knowledge of English on the other side (which is never acknowledged), with several silent listeners and note-takers in attendance. Every visit, even to a museum or the zoo, has to be arranged in advance; there is no such thing as going anywhere unannounced. The manner is polite, never peremptory, and one's permanent escorts are likable people who try genuinely to meet one's desires if they can. When one finds, after judicial testing, just the right balance between acquiescence and demand, they can even be flexible. When we asked for a day on our own in Yenan, which is small enough to find one's way around without getting lost, they made no objection.

Here we made a significant finding. We blundered into the courtyard of the local high school where we watched rehearsals of a dance-drama, gymnastics on the playground, and were invited by smiles and gestures into the reading room. It was the only institution unalerted to our coming that we managed to visit. In the fact that nothing was notably different or deficient in comparison with the planned visits to pre-selected schools lies the significance. What the Revolution and the Communist regime have accomplished for the revival and rehabilitation of China and for the material welfare, dignity, and political participation of the people speaks for itself. Visitors do not need to be carefully steered and shepherded to see that.

Chinese officialdom, however, will doubtless continue to insist on control, not only because it is in the nature of the Marxist system but because it is in their blood. In China's past the chief obstacle to normal relations with the outside world was the refusal to receive foreigners as equals and the insubstantial belief that China could control access under a set of absurd regulations and impossible restrictions. What the Westerners wanted at first was not dominion but trade. If China had opened her ports to begin with, there might have been no Opium Wars. Thereafter her contact with foreigners became one of forced penetration, concessions, unequal treaties, patronage by missionaries, and the humiliation of being treated by the whites as "natives." In the twentieth century China became the victim of Japan, a suppliant for Western aid, an unequal ally in World War II, and finally the betrayed partner of the chief Marxist power. Given this history, one would hardly expect to find an easy relationship with foreigners.

Nor should we expect to find a greater understanding of Western mental habits than we have traditionally shown for theirs. Never having been a democracy, China has only the most nominal understanding of the principles of democratic government. Recently disliking some articles in the British press, Peking lodged a protest in London. When the Foreign Office endeavored to explain the limits of its influence on a free press, the Chinese Ambassador brushed aside the disclaimer, saying, "You must take effective measures."

The fanciful explanations and evasions which are meant to be understood as "No" or "No comment" or "Don't pursue this further" are another source of difficulty. The Chinese consider failure to accept these circumlocutions as bad manners while the Westerner considers their transparent nonsense an insult to his intelligence. When he is told that he cannot go from Sian to Loyang on the same east-west railway line without returning to Peking 550 miles to the north, and he insists on a reason, he is disinclined to accept meekly the explanation that there is no toilet on the Sian-Loyang train. When after vain requests to see the Yellow River at various points, he is told that the drive cannot be arranged from Sian because the great bend of the river is 350 kilometers away, and he unforgivably gets out his map and demonstrates the distance to be under 150 kilometers, the procedure on neither side is the best path to friendship.

When the Westerner, to make conversation at a banquet with the Vice-Chairman of the Provincial Revolutionary Committee of Shensi, brings up the name of the famous "Christian General," Feng Yu-hsiang, governor and warlord of Shensi for a quarter century preceding the Communists, and the Vice-Chairman replies flatly, "Feng Yu-hsiang was never governor or warlord of Shensi," one is left bewildered. It is as if Mayor Lindsay looking one straight in the eye were to say, "Fiorello La Guardia? No, he was never mayor of New York." What motivated the Vice-Chairman of Shensi to make his assertion I have no idea. I could only feel myself facing a cultural gap without a bridge.

The future of relations is clearly not without pitfalls, but the opportunity now to establish a workable relationship is probably as good as it is likely to be—if for no other reason than China's extreme bitterness toward Russia. The rise of acute hostility between the two Communist giants is one of those turns in human affairs that happily make fools of the dogmatists, and history eternally fascinating. It has redirected the course of the last quarter of our century and, as a case of hate and fear in one quarter causing détente elsewhere, it has brought good out of bad to confuse the sentimentalists and inspire philosophers.

The hostility arose on the one side from the Soviet Union's jealousy, gradually becoming apprehension, of a younger rival's challenge to its supremacy over the Communist world, and on the other side from China's mixed dependence on Soviet assistance, mistrust of Soviet ambitions, and resentment of Soviet dictation. Physical contiguity and a disputed frontier exacerbated these mutual sentiments. When the Russians decided that in assisting China's nuclear development, they were creating a potential threat to themselves, they broke it off midway and withdrew all industrial aid. Left to their own technology with unfinished installations, the Chinese felt the fury of the betrayed. Mention Russia and they talk first of "broken contracts"; orthodox scorn of "revisionists" and "socialist-imperialists" comes second. Since the break, the Russians have moved what appears to be a permanent force of a million men up against the frontier with the result that both nations live in the paranoid shadow of war—the Russians tempted by the idea of a preemptive strike, the Chinese preparing for it. Not without reason it has been said that for China, Nixon's visit was equivalent in worrying the Russians to a million men on China's side of the frontier. Meanwhile the Chinese feel forced to turn their energies into building underground cities which, it is claimed, could save a quarter of the population in the event of nuclear attack.

With the other super-power allied to Chiang Kai-shek and represented by a belligerent American presence off Formosa and on the Asiatic mainland, China understandably felt encircled prior to 1971. It is this situation that explains the heavy internal propaganda on armed force and the glory of the gun and the heroic virtues of the PLA. Reaching down to primary schoolchildren who conduct military games and exercises with mock rifles, it is designed to instill military self-confidence and dignify the formerly despised status of the soldier. The purpose is more defensive than aggressive. As a Socialist state, the Chinese seem genuinely convinced of their own non-aggressiveness. The Socialist system, they maintain, does not allow invasion of other countries. "How could we explain to the world if we engaged in aggression against another state?" Since the party line establishes the equal status of all nations, China according to this dogma can never become a super-power because it will never dominate others. Similar assertions about non-interference in the affairs of others are less convincing.

The one people whom the Chinese seem to exclude from the unity of the masses and regard as somehow undetachable from their government are the Israelis, the world's eternal exception. No doubt this can be explained as a matter of wooing the Arabs away from the Russians, yet the Chinese show a particular animus in this case that is surprising, especially as Israel is the enemy of their enemy and is similar to them in many ways that might be expected to evoke empathy. They are the two oldest peoples with a continuous history and a continuous language and the only two now maintaining sovereignty over the same territory as 3,000 years ago. Both went through a long struggle and a final armed fight to achieve that sovereignty, both came to power at about the same time, 1948–49, both pursued a dominant idea, in one case revival, in the other revolution. Socialism if not Marxism was the early Zionist goal, and the communal system of the kibbutzim antedates the present communes of China. Both nations stress self-sufficiency for similar reasons, and both live in fear of invasion.

To test the reaction, I attempted once or twice to bring out this likeness and suggest that China could exercise a unique influence in the Middle East that might make a major contribution to world peace. The reaction was not a bland pretense that I was talking about the weather which is the usual Chinese way of avoiding an uncomfortable subject, but an angry rejection of any likeness to "imperialist" Israel. In the case of a reasonably sophisticated diplomat like Huang Hua, chief of the Chinese delegation to the UN, it elicited a fiery denunciation of Israel as "the tool of American oil interests," a twist that would make even Aramco laugh. One never knows, when the Chinese talk like this, whether it is ignorance, or befuddled Marxist orthodoxy, or some kind of reverse oriental version of reality.

From the point of view of a single, unofficial, necessarily superficial traveler, these are some of the factors that will enter into the process of forging a Sino-American relationship. The relationship is of large importance to both countries, not to mention the world, but I do not think it should be approached sentimentally or with too great expectations. The Chinese are not likely, I expect, soon to expand very appreciably the admission of foreigners although the pressure on their doors is going to be hard to resist, as it was before, and may compel some relaxation of their tight system of selection. The given excuse of limited facilities is not determining; in an authoritarian state facilities are expandable but "friendships" must be supervised, and China intends to ensure that these develop according to her design.

On our side there are problems too. Vis-à-vis

Communist China, our heterodox political opinions make some of us too starry-eyed and others too hard-nosed. Anti-Communism has conditioned our foreign and military policy for too long not to have cut a deep channel. McCarthyism is never dead in this country, a fact too little appreciated by the Chinese, themselves suffering from a sentimental illusion about the masses being always right. They fail to realize that a large proportion of Americans firmly regard "Commy bastard" as one word and Communism as the source of all evil from long hair to crime, and are not so much bemused by a reactionary government as ahead of it.

What one would like to hope for from our side is good will and a cool realism; a recognition that Communist China has different needs, different goals, and a different outlook on the world from ours and has committed itself to a political system which may be antithetical but need not be inimical. On that understanding we could move toward a reasonably sound relationship, not forgetting that "friendship is a form of struggle, too."

IF MAO HAD
COME TO
WASHINGTON
IN 1945

An Essay in Alternatives

If Mao Had Come
to Washington in 1945

An Essay in Alternatives

ONE of the great "ifs" and harsh ironies of history hangs on the fact that in January 1945, four and a half years before they achieved national power in China, Mao Tse-tung and Chou En-lai, in an effort to establish a working relationship with the United States, offered to come to Washington to talk in person with President Roosevelt. What became of the offer has been a mystery until, with the declassification of new material, we now know for the first time that the United States made no response to the overture. Twenty-seven years, two wars, and x million lives later, after immeasurable harm wrought by the mutual suspicion and phobia of two great powers not on speaking terms, an American President, reversing the unmade journey of 1945, has traveled to Peking to treat with the same two Chinese leaders. Might the interim have been otherwise?

The original proposal, transmitted on January 9 by Major Ray Cromley, Acting Chief of the American Military Observers Mission then in Yenan, to the Headquarters of General Albert C. Wedemeyer in Chungking, stated that Mao and Chou wanted their request to be sent to the "highest United States officials." The text * was as follows:

> Yenan Government wants [to] dispatch to America an unofficial rpt unofficial group to interpret and explain to American civilians and officials interested the present situation and problems of China. Next is strictly off record suggestion by same: Mao and Chou will be immediately available either singly or together for exploratory conference at Washington should President Roosevelt express desire to receive them at White House as leaders of a primary Chinese party.

Chou requested air travel to the United States if the invitation from Roosevelt were forthcoming. In case it was not, Mao and Chou wanted their request to remain secret in order to protect their relationship with Chiang Kai-shek, which was then in the throes of negotiation.

* The author wishes to acknowledge with thanks the assistance of Mr. Ray Cromley and Mr. John S. Service who supplied information and elucidation, and of Mr. William Cunliffe of the Military Records Division, National Archives, who found and secured declassification of the relevant documents, viz. Nos. 322 and 324 from Dixie Mission to Chungking; Nos. 21084 and 25246 from Marshall to Wedemeyer; Wedemeyer's replies to Marshall of 22 and 27 January 1945; and the undated typewritten draft of the first of these. I am also indebted to Mr. J. C. James of the Roosevelt Library at Hyde Park for several searches, both negative and positive.

The message, received in Chungking on January 10, was not forwarded, except as secondary reference in another context, either to the President, the State Department, or the War Department. It was held up in Chungking by Ambassador Patrick J. Hurley with the arm-twisted concurrence of General Wedemeyer.

Before examining the circumstances and reasons for this procedure, let us imagine instead that, following a more normal process, the message had been duly forwarded to the "highest officials," and had received an affirmative response which is 99 and 44/100 percent unlikely but not absolutely impossible. If Mao and Chou had then gone to Washington, if they had succeeded in persuading Roosevelt of the real and growing strength of their sub-government relative to that of the decadent Central Government, and if they had gained what they came for—some supply of arms, a cessation of America's unqualified commitment to Chiang Kai-shek, and firm American pressure on Chiang to admit the Communists on acceptable terms to a coalition government (a base from which they expected to expand)—what then would have been the consequences?

With prestige and power enhanced by an American connection, the Communists' rise and the Kuomintang's demise, both by then inevitable, would have been accelerated. Three years of civil war in a country desperately weary of war and misgovernment might have been, if not entirely averted, certainly curtailed. The United States, in that case guiltless of prolonging the civil war by consistently aiding the certain loser, would not then have aroused the profound antagonism of the ultimate winner. This antagonism would not then have been expressed in the arrest, beating, and in some cases imprisonment and deportation of American consular officials, the seizure of our consulate in Mukden, and other harassments, and these acts in turn might not then have decided us in anger against recognition of the Communist government. If, in the absence of ill-feeling, we had established relations on some level with the People's Republic, permitting communication in a crisis, and if the Chinese had not been moved by hate and suspicion of us to make common cause with the Soviet Union, it is conceivable that there might have been no Korean War with all its evil consequences. From that war rose the twin specters of an expansionist Chinese Communism and an indivisible Sino-Soviet partnership. Without those two concepts to addle statesmen and nourish demagogues, our history, our present, and our future, would have been different. We might not have come to Vietnam.

II

Although every link in this chain is an "if," together they tell us something about the conduct and the quirks of American foreign policy. What

we have to ask is whether the quirks were acci-
dents only, or was the bent built in? Was there a
real alternative or was the outcome ineluctable?
Looking back to find the answer, one perceives
the ghost of the present, and from the perspective
of a quarter-century's distance, its outline is more
clearly visible than among the too-near trees of
the Pentagon Papers.

In the circumstances of 1945 there are three
main points to remember: first, the Japanese were
as yet undefeated; second, American policy was
concentrated urgently and almost obsessively on
the need to bring Nationalists and Communists
into some form of coalition; third, the American
Military Observers Mission of nine, later enlarged
to eighteen members (known as the Dixie Mission), was already in contact with the Communists,
having been functioning in Yenan since July 1944.
Its purpose was to organize an intelligence net-
work using Communist men and facilities in a
strategic area vital to future operations, and generally to assess Communist capabilities and aims.
These had become acutely important with the approach of an American landing in China (at that
time still contemplated as part of the final assault),
and with the approach, too, of Russian entry
against Japan.

Coalition was the central factor in American
plans because only in this way would it be possible, while still supporting the legal government,
to utilize Communist forces and territory against

the Japanese entrenched in the north. A patched-up unity was the more imperative from our point of view because of the need to avert civil war between the Chinese parties. This above all else was the thing we most feared because it could defeat our major objective, a stable, united China after the war—and because civil chaos would tempt outsiders. If the conflict erupted before the Japanese had been defeated and repatriated, they might take advantage of it to dig themselves into the mainland. And then there was the looming shadow of the Soviet Union. In the absence of coalition, we feared the Russians might use their influence, when they entered the war, to stir up the Communists and increase the possibility of a disunited China afterward. As early as May 1941, it may be worth noting, an unpublished policy study of the Council on Foreign Relations on the interrelation of the Chinese Communists, Japan, and the Soviet Union, stated: "It is vital that there be no civil war in China."

During November and December 1944, negotiations for coalition were pursued by Ambassador Hurley as go-between, with optimism, enthusiasm, and a minimum of acquaintance with the causes, nature, and history of the problem. On November 10 he had succeeded in hammering out with the Communists a Five-Point Plan for their participation in a coalition government. Its terms would have allowed them relative freedom of political action while acknowledging Chiang's leadership and joint authority over their armed forces. Because Mao and his colleagues saw coalition as an avenue to American aid and, in the long run, to national power, they were prepared to pay this temporary price. To Hurley, who thought the Communists were a kind of Chinese populist Farmer-Labor party whose aim was a democratic share in national government, the terms seemed so workable and such a triumph of his own diplomacy that he signed the document along with Mao.

On November 16, to his dismay, Chiang Kai-shek rejected the plan in toto on the ground, as he told Hurley, that to admit the Communists to government on the terms Hurley had signed would eventually result in their taking control of it. Hurley, who identified the Generalissimo's tenure with American interest—and with his own—was ready at once to adapt coalition to the Generalissimo's terms. That these did not reflect the realities in China was not apparent to the Ambassador, although it was to his staff, who had been observing conditions under the Kuomintang for years and now had the opportunity to visit and investigate the Communist zone. Their assessment pointed to a different American interest, and this became the critical issue: Was the American objective preservation of the Generalissimo, or was it a wider option that would not involve us in the fate of a "steadily decaying regime"?

Hurley and Wedemeyer were convinced converts of the first thesis. It was not easy at that time to envisage China without Chiang Kai-shek. His towering reputation as national leader made it an article of faith to most outsiders that no one else could hold China together and that his fall would carry chaos in its wake. It was easy for Hurley and Wedemeyer to believe in him: the trappings of power are very persuasive. Both the new ambassador and the new commander were ambitious to show how they could succeed where General Stilwell had failed and both saw the obvious path to success as keeping in step with the Generalissimo.

Pressed by Hurley into making a counteroffer to the Communists, Chiang proposed a plan of coalition which would bring the Communist armed forces under Nationalist control and in return legalize the Communists as a party. Hurley promptly espoused the Generalissimo's plan although it nullified the terms he had negotiated with Mao, and exerted his most strenuous efforts, assisted by Wedemeyer, to persuade the Communists to accept it. They naturally refused an arrangement which would have meant submission, not coalition. Concluding that negotiations through a mediator who had committed himself to the other side were useless, they broke off the talks, and from that time on ceased to trust Hurley. When Wedemeyer argued that if they came to terms with the Generalissimo the United States could send them arms and supplies, they were not persuaded because they knew Chiang would control the distribution.

When Hurley offered to revisit Yenan to resume the talks, he was turned down, and when Colonel David D. Barrett, Chief of the Dixie Mission, was asked to add his persuasion, he was told by Mao and Chou that they still hoped for and needed American arms but not on Chiang's terms. They said the United States was propping up a "rotten shell" in Chiang Kai-shek, who, in spite of all the United States might do, was "doomed to failure." Barrett left the interview feeling he had talked to two leaders who were "absolutely sure of the strength of their position."

Negotiations were thus deadlocked, leaving the Communists, who had made a serious effort from which they had hoped to gain much, in need of a new approach. Haphazardly at this point certain exploratory and apparently unconcerted overtures from American military sources were made to them which left them encouraged but confused. The proposals were brought on December 15 by Colonel Barrett, and simultaneously but separately by Colonel Willis H. Bird, Deputy Chief of OSS (Office of Strategic Services) in China. Both projects concerned possible airborne landings of American technical units to operate jointly with Communist forces. Colonel Bird's plan, which was the more grandiose, involved the "complete co-operation" of all Communist armed forces "when strategic use required" by the American command. Whether this plan was intended to bypass the Generalissimo or whether Colonel Bird had ever considered this aspect of the problem is not mentioned in his rather jaunty report, which does, however, make the claim that "Theater Command already agreed on principle of support to fullest extent of Communists. . . ."

Colonel Barrett brought two proposals authorized by Wedemeyer's Chief of Staff, General Robert B. McClure. McClure had cleared the first one, limited to 4,000 to 5,000 American technical troops, with General Chen Cheng, the Generalissimo's Chief of Staff, and secured the kind of ambiguous reply which a Chinese uses to disguise "No" and an American takes to mean "Maybe." The second more startling proposal on December 27 carried McClure's verbal assurance to Barrett that it had been cleared with Ambassador Hurley. It projected, after victory in Europe, a beachhead on Shantung and the landing of an entire U.S. paratroop division of some 28,000 men for whom the Communists were asked if they could take care of supplies, other than arms and ammunition, until U.S. Army supply procedures could begin to function. They said they could, although Barrett could not help wondering whether, behind Chinese composure, they might not have been slightly dazed by the responsibility and its implications.

Faced by such prospects, uncertain how far they were authorized at the summit, the Communists understandably felt a need for clarification by direct contact in Washington, bypassing Hurley.

More than clarification, what they wanted was recognition. The offer to make the distant journey—which would have been Mao's first outside China—was a measure of their seriousness. Today, after twenty-five years of Mao's vicious denunciations of the United States as the fixed—and doomed—enemy of the Socialist camp (matched by vintage Dulles, early Nixon, and others from our side), the obvious question is: Were the Chinese Communists ideologically still sufficiently flexible in 1945 really to desire an association with the United States?

III

Before everything else the Chinese Communists were pragmatic. Ideological purity having proved nearly fatal in the 1920s, they had learned to adapt political action to present fact, and were ready to deal, for survival or advantage, with whatever ideological opponent the situation required. If they could deal with Chiang Kai-shek, as they had in 1936 and were prepared to again, why not the United States? What they hoped to gain can be reconstructed from the frank conversations held by Mao and Chou with John S. Service, political officer of the Dixie Mission, who reported them at length.

Primarily they wanted to convince President Roosevelt that they, not the Kuomintang, represented the future of China. They knew that time was working in their favor, that the mandate of heaven was slowly and irresistibly shifting. If they could somehow make this plain at the policy-making level in Washington, then the United States might be persuaded to mitigate its support of Chiang and thus hasten the shift. Second, they wanted access, as a partner in a coalition government, to American arms and other munitions on the model of Tito, their Communist counterpart in Europe. On the basis of usefulness against the enemy, they considered they had no less a claim. Armament was their most serious deficiency; they had gained control of North China beyond and behind Japanese lines by an astonishing organization but without enough weapons to risk a real battle. In Washington they hoped to persuade the President of the validity of their claim. They felt the United States was blind to the real state of the Kuomintang's decline and their own rise, and that if they could reach Roosevelt they could make this clear.

Roosevelt's aura as a man with sympathy for the oppressed had penetrated the remotest corners of the world. In *Christ Stopped at Eboli*, Carlo Levi tells how, on entering a hovel in a miserable village in God-forsaken Calabria, he was confronted on the wall by a crucifix, a picture of the family's absent son, and a picture of Roosevelt. While it is doubtful if, apart from propaganda posters of the four Allied leaders, the American President appeared on any private walls of Yenan, he was present in the minds of the leaders. On Roosevelt's re-election in 1944, Mao sent him a message of congratulations and received a reply in which Roosevelt said he looked forward to "vigorous co-operation with all the Chinese forces" against the common enemy, Japan. If not definitive, this was at least an opening.

The American observers in Yenan found their hosts intensely curious about the United States, anxious to learn what they could of means and techniques, especially military, developed by the Americans. Mao, according to Major Cromley, "would grab intellectually anything about the United States that anyone could tell him." He and his colleagues had been impressed by the steady advance of American forces in the extraordinarily difficult campaign across the Pacific, and they realized it was this that would be the main force in the defeat of the Japanese homeland. In the real world in which they now had to make their way, the United States with its money, its resources, and its current presence in Asia was the country they had to deal with—for the interim.

"We can risk no conflict," Mao told Service, "with the United States." They were not concerned about adulteration by a rival ideology because they were confident of the ultimate victory of their own. They wanted American recognition of what they had accomplished and were capable of accomplishing and thus recognition as a major party, not an outlaw. They wanted to acquire belligerent status as a party to the coming Allied victory so that they could not be ignored in the arrangements for postwar China, nor in the organization of the United Nations. And certainly they had in mind that an American connection would help them to meet that none-too-welcome day when the heavy tramp of the Soviet Union should enter Manchuria. In short, they wanted to find out at the source whether, if Chiang continued to refuse coalition, there was "any chance," as Mao asked Service, "of American support of the Chinese Communist Party?" They wanted to know where they stood.

The governing factor was that in their own minds they fully expected to succeed to the sovereignty of China. Here lay the problem which in the Communists' relation to the United States eventually became the shipwreck rock. The Communist view of it was made explicit by Mao as early as August 1944: "For America to give arms only to the Kuomintang will in its effect be interference because it will enable the Kuomintang to oppose the will of the people of China." While this may have been a subjective judgment of the will of the people, it was more realistic than otherwise, and recognized as such by American observers whose duty was to assess the evidence. As "the only group in China possessing a program with positive appeal to the people," reported John P. Davies, second secretary of the Embassy who was attached as political officer to the Theater Command, the Communists were the first group in modern Chinese history to have "positive and wide-spread popular support. . . . China's destiny is not Chiang's but theirs." He thought this was a consideration that the United States in seeking to determine policy should keep in mind.

The tenor of advice by our career officers both in China and the State Department at this time was that unqualified support of Chiang Kai-shek was not the best means of achieving unity in China. By encouraging in Chiang a false sense of his own strength, it made him intransigent to compromise and therefore more likely to precipitate civil war than prevent it. The staff in China felt that we should retain our freedom to establish contact with the Communists, who were certain to retain North China and very likely inherit Manchuria after the war, because only through U.S. contact and economic aid could we keep them out of the coming Soviet embrace. The plea of officers in the field for greater "flexibility of approach" grew almost impassioned. Sustaining Chiang should not become, as one said, "an end in itself." The China Affairs and Far East divisions of the Department tried to convey the voice of the field upward to the policy-making level, even to the point of suggesting that if Chiang himself did not take remedial action, a re-examination of U.S. policy would not only be justified but "very likely imperative."

The difficulty was the not unusual one in the conduct of American foreign policy, that the voice of the field was not reaching, or certainly not influencing, the ear at the policy-making level—in this case the President. Out of an old prejudice against career diplomats, justifiable almost anywhere but in China, Roosevelt always felt he would be better informed by a personal envoy—in this case Ambassador Hurley.

IV

The personality of Hurley is a major quirk in this history. One would like to think that historical factors were more rooted in natural law, more Toynbeean in scope, than the chance character of a minor individual who was neither heroic nor demonic. But history is not law-abiding or orderly and will often respond to a breeze as carelessly as a leaf upon a lake.

It happened that Hurley was a man whose conceit, ambition, and very vulnerable ego were wrapped up in his mission to the point of frenzy. From birth in a miner's cabin in Oklahoma, he had risen through a Horatio Alger boyhood to the practice of law and a lucrative representation of the oil interests of the Choctaw Indians. A later client was Sinclair Oil. He made a fortune of $15,000,000, served overseas in World War I, became Hoover's Secretary of War, and coated the rough ebullience of a frontier background with the glossy Republicanism of Andrew Mellon. Tall, handsome, and impressive, he dressed with the care of a Beau

Brummell and when ordered to wear civilian clothes as Ambassador could only be induced to shed a general's uniform and medals on the direct intervention of the President. Vanity was Hurley's security blanket.

His initial assignment to China as special envoy to facilitate the appointment of General Stilwell as Commander in Chief of China's armed forces had ended in a notable reverse. Instead of Hurley's cajoling Chiang, Chiang had cajoled Hurley into supporting his demand for Stilwell's recall. Hurley therefore felt a double need to make a success of coalition. He had wrecked his chances as mediator, however, by allying himself with the Generalissimo for the sake of the ambassadorship. Hurley was just what Chiang wanted in an envoy—a man with direct access to the President and no experience of China, who was easy to manipulate through his vanity. When Ambassador Clarence E. Gauss resigned at the time of Stilwell's departure, Chiang was only too pleased to ask for Hurley as successor. In a personal message to Roosevelt (sent via T. V. Soong to Harry Hopkins, avoiding the State Department), he solicited a "more permanent" mission for Hurley who "has my complete confidence" in dealing with the Communists, and would thus be able to make a contribution to the war effort by solving the problem of coalition. Roosevelt was lured; he believed in the efficacy of harmony. If nothing else had worked in China, maybe a person pleasing to Chiang Kai-shek might. Hurley received the appointment and owed it to Chiang.

As a result, he at once convinced himself that his mission and the policy of the United States ("my policy" as he sometimes called it) were to "prevent the collapse of the National Government" and "to sustain Chiang Kai-shek as President of the Republic and Generalissimo of the Armies." No such instructions appear in the documents, and despite Hurley's later claims, they could hardly have been oral since he was in China when he was appointed. It should be added, however, that when he stated this understanding of his mission in a rare communication to the State Department, no one disabused him. This was partly because the Department had no rein on Hurley, who generally bypassed it, and partly because it was unable to decide, except in noble generalizations, exactly what our China policy was. And no one knew for sure what it was in the President's mind.

Before he ever reached China, Hurley's estimate of the situation was shaped by the premise, which he accepted without question because it was told to him personally by Molotov, that the Soviet Union was not interested in the Chinese Communists, who were not really Communists at all. He thereafter underestimated them, said their strength and popular support were greatly exaggerated, and insisted that as soon as they were convinced that the Soviet Union would not support them, they would settle with the National Government and be content with minority status. Coalition would be easy. "There is very little difference, if any," he reported, between the "avowed principles" of the Kuomintang and the Communists; both "are striving for democratic principles." This may well be the least sophisticated statement ever made by an American ambassador. It reflects the characteristic American refusal to recognize the existence of fundamental divergence; hence the American assumption that there is nothing that cannot be negotiated.

Hurley accepted no guidance from his staff. Because he was over his head in the ancient and entangled circumstances which he proposed to settle, he fiercely resented and rejected the counsel of anyone more knowledgeable about China than himself. When the coalition blew up in his face and he found Chinese affairs resisting his finesse, depriving him of the diplomatic success he had counted on, he could find an explanation only in a paranoid belief that he was the victim of a plot by disloyal subordinates. He did not consider there might be a Chinese reason.

On the premise that his mission was to sustain Chiang Kai-shek, Hurley of course blocked the bid of Mao and Chou to go to Washington, the more so as it was intended to bypass himself. Although their message had been addressed to Wedemeyer for just that reason, it reached Hurley because Wedemeyer was absent in Burma at the time, and he and Hurley had an agreement to share all incoming information. A second message from Yenan the next day, addressed to Wedemeyer on an "eyes alone" basis, quoted Chou En-lai as specifically stating that "General Hurley must not get this information as I don't trust his discretion." This, too, reached Hurley with effect that can be imagined. At the same time he learned through information passed by Nationalist agents in Yenan of Bird's and Barrett's military proposals to the Communists. A terrible bell rang in his mind: here was the reason that the Communists had walked out on coalition. They had received a direct offer and were already secretly proposing to go to Washington over his head!

Barrett's proposals had, of course, emanated from Theater Command but Hurley ignored that out of his need to find some conspiratorial reason for the breakdown of coalition. Wrathfully claiming that Bird and Barrett had acted without authority, he informed the President on January 14 that their action had become known to him only when it "was made apparent by the Communists applying to Wedemeyer to secure secret passage for Mao Tse-tung and Chou En-lai to Washington for a conference with you."

Only in this context (repeated in a second telegram of February 7) was Roosevelt informed of the Communist request. It appeared as no more than a by-product of unwarranted action by American officers undermining Hurley's efforts for coalition.* The plan for military co-operation with Yenan, Hurley said, would constitute "recognition of the Communist Party as an armed belligerent," and lead to "destruction of the National Government . . . chaos and civil war, and a defeat of America's policy in China." In the meantime, he assured Roosevelt, by discovering and frustrating the Communists' maneuver, he had now prevailed upon Chou En-lai to return to Chungking to resume negotiations.

V

What of the receiving end? The Communist request reached Roosevelt in terms already condemned by his ambassador. It reached him, moreover, when he was plunged into preparations for the Yalta conference and overwhelmed by the dismaying problems of approaching victory. (Hurley's second, fuller telegram arrived after the President had already left Washington for Yalta.) War crimes, the postwar treatment of Germany, the Soviet claim to sixteen seats in the United Nations,

* Hurley's accusations, passed on by the White House to General Marshall and by him in a peremptory query to Wedemeyer, caused a furious quarrel between Wedemeyer and Hurley, followed by an enforced agreement between them on an explanation for Marshall that would leave Wedemeyer's command blameless while not disputing Hurley. This was accomplished in a convoluted masterpiece covering everybody except Colonel Barrett, who had neglected the soldier's elementary precaution of obtaining his orders in writing. At Hurley's insistence, unopposed by Wedemeyer,

the Polish border, the arrest of Badoglio, trouble in Yugoslavia and Greece, the fall of the Iranian government, not to mention the necessity, according to Secretary Edward Stettinius, of a "private talk with Mr. Churchill on British meat purchases in Argentina"—all these in the thirteenth year of a crisis-filled presidency did not leave Roosevelt eager to precipitate a new crisis with the unmanageable Chiang Kai-shek.

Bewildered by the intractability of China, disenchanted with the Generalissimo but fearful of the troubles that would rush in if the United States relaxed support, Roosevelt was inclined to look for a solution in the coming conference with Russia. His hope was to secure Stalin's agreement to support the Nationalist government, thus giving the Chinese Communists no choice but unity. He succeeded in obtaining the desired agreement at Yalta and returned to be confronted by a choice in our China policy. Tired, ill, and in the last month of life, he made a decision that closed this episode.

Coalition having reached another deadlock, Hurley and Wedemeyer arrived in Washington in March 1945 for consultation. Choosing their presence there as the opportunity to bring to a head the issue in American policy, all the political officers of the Embassy in Chungking, led by the

---

Barrett's nomination for promotion to Brigadier General, which had already gone forward, was withdrawn. His was the first in a line of honorable careers damaged to fill the need for scapegoats in China.

Chargé d'Affaires, George Atcheson, joined in an unprecedented action. With the concurrence and "strong approval" of Wedemeyer's Chief of Staff, they addressed a long telegram to the Department, in effect condemning the Ambassador's policy. It pointed out that the Communists represented a force in China that was on the rise, that it was "dangerous to American interests from the long-range point of view" to be precluded from dealing with them, that with the approach of a landing in China the time was short before we would have to decide whether to co-operate with them or not. They recommended therefore "that the President inform the Generalissimo in definite terms that military necessity requires that we supply and co-operate with the Communists," and that such decision "will not be delayed or contingent upon" coalition.

After precipitating the explosive reaction of Hurley, who could see only an "act of disloyalty" to himself, the telegram was submitted to the President with the Department's recommendation that it provided an opportunity to re-examine the whole situation and "in particular" the possibility of "giving war supplies to the Chinese Communists as well as to Chiang Kai-shek." The President discussed it in two conversations with Hurley on March 8 and 24, with no officer of the State Department recorded as present on either occasion. Hurley evidently argued convincingly that the Russian agreement secured by the President at Yalta would sufficiently weaken the Communists so that he could promise unity in China by "the end of April," as he had already told the Department. Roosevelt, clinging to the goal he had started with and ever the optimist, decided in favor of Hurley's policy of dealing exclusively with the Generalissimo and of making no connection with the Communists without his consent. In effect this rejected the recommendation of the Embassy staff and left the conduct of American policy to the tyro Ambassador. Thus confirmed, Hurley was able to insist on his requirement that Atcheson and his colleagues involved in the Embassy telegram, five out of six of them Chinese-speaking and representing nine decades of Chinese experience, should be transferred out of China. This was duly accomplished on Hurley's return.*

* Morale at the Embassy having sunk low under the effect of Hurley's rages and vendettas, the officers on duty in Chungking, whose careers were vulnerable to unfavorable action by the Chief of Mission, were anxious to be transferred, or in the case of two who were on leave in the United States, not to return. Atcheson, as Hurley's ranking subordinate, though too senior to be adversely affected, could not remain under the Ambassador's violent objection, and was transferred to General MacArthur's command as Political Adviser. Hurley personally obtained the removal of Service whom he correctly guessed to be the principal drafter of the telegram, by direct request to Secretary of War Henry L. Stimson (Service being attached to the Military Command). In the case of Raymond Ludden, a political officer who had also served with the Dixie Mission and after a four-month tour of Communist territory had reported the likelihood of their coming to power, Hurley obtained a statement from Wedemeyer that he "no longer required Ludden's services." Fulton Freeman, third secretary of the

In making his choice the President undoubtedly believed or was persuaded by Hurley that it would compel the Communists to accept Chiang's terms for coalition. But it was only possible to believe this by rejecting the Embassy's appraisal of the seriousness and the dynamism of the Communist challenge. The choice was the last important decision of Roosevelt's life. A few days later he left for Warm Springs where he died.

In March when the President made this decision, Mao and Chou in conversations with Service were still emphasizing and amplifying their desire for co-operation and friendship with the United States. The rebuff suffered by the lack of any reply to their offer to go to Washington was never mentioned (doubtless because they wished to keep it secret), and in fact none of the political officers attached to the Dixie Mission knew anything about it. Supported by Chu Teh, Liu Shao-chi, and other leaders of the Party, Mao and Chou returned repeatedly to the theme that China and the United States complemented each other economically—in China's need for postwar economic development and America's ability to assist and participate in it.

Embassy, Japan Language Officer Yuni, and Arthur Ringwalt, former Consul in Kweilin recently transferred to Chungking, who suffered the longest under Hurley's vindictiveness, were all variously reassigned. With the exception of Atcheson, who died shortly thereafter, the careers of all these men were slowed or otherwise damaged to greater or less degree by this episode. (Information supplied to the author by John S. Service.)

Trying to assess how far this represented genuine conviction, Service concluded that Mao was certainly sincere in hoping to avoid an exclusive dependence on the Soviet Union.

The banishment shortly afterward of Service and the others concerned in the Atcheson telegram was a signal to the Communists of the American choice. In reaction, their first overt signs of hostility appeared in the form of articles by Mao in the Communist press. Confined so far to attacks on the "Hurley policy," these seemed still to retain hope of a change by Roosevelt's successor. In his speech to the Seventh Party Congress in June, Mao seemed to be half warning, half pleading. If the pro-Chiang choice by "a group of people in the U.S. government" were to prevail, he said, it would drag the American government "into the deep stinking cesspool of Chinese reaction" and "place a crushing burden on the government and people of the United States and plunge them into endless woes and troubles."

After V-J Day American forces enabled the Nationalists, who had neither the means nor the plans ready for the occasion, to take the Japanese surrender on the mainland and regain the occupied cities. The United States moved its marine forces into the important northern cities and ports (Tientsin, Tsingtao, Peking, Chingwangtao) to deny these centers and the railroads in the area to the Communists until Chiang's troops, ferried by

American ships and planes, could get there. To the Communists this constituted clear intervention since their own forces would otherwise have re-occupied the north. Though justified by us under the pressing necessity of disarming the Japanese, our action was a logical development of the decision to sustain Chiang, and was taken as such by the Communists. Confirmed, as they saw it, by the United Nations Relief and Rehabilitation Administration's discrimination against Communist areas and by American toleration of Japanese troops serving with the Nationalists, they took the turn toward antagonism which in the course of the next four years was to become definitive.

Through 1945 efforts for coalition, mediated by Hurley, continued—largely because neither side wished to appear to have chosen the course of civil war—but they were empty of intent. Failing to move either side any closer to the unity he had so often and so confidently promised, Hurley grew increasingly erratic and disturbed and suddenly resigned in November 1945 with a famous blast, the first salvo of McCarthyism. His mission had been thwarted, he claimed, by a section of the State Department which was "endeavoring to support Communism generally as well as specifically in China." He could not admit, and perhaps never understood, that his own estimate of the situation had been inadequate and the current of Chinese affairs simply too strong for him.

VI

Beyond Hurley, responsibility lay with the President. Hindsight makes his rejection of the Embassy's advice appear shortsighted, but every historical act is entitled to be examined in the light of the circumstances that surrounded it. Without doubt the primary factor influencing him was the Russian agreement obtained at Yalta. Both Roosevelt and Hurley believed that the Soviet Union held the key and that its still secret pledge to enter a treaty of alliance with Chiang Kai-shek (subsequently fulfilled in August) would in its effect on both sides in China serve to block the danger of civil war.

This belief was made possible only by underestimating the Communists as a *Chinese* phenomenon with roots reaching down into a hundred years of unmet needs and strength drawn from the native necessity of revolution. Back in 1930 Ambassador Nelson Johnson, a man of no unusual powers but able to observe the obvious, reported that Communism was not the cause of chaos in China but rather the effect of "certain fundamental conditions." One such small voice, however, was overwhelmed as time went on by the conventional wisdom which held, first, that the Chinese would never accept Communism because it was incompatible with the structure of Chinese society, and second, according to the Molotov dictum which much impressed Roosevelt, that the Chinese Communists were not Communists at all. On these premises it was easy to persuade oneself that the Communists were not the coming rulers of China but a party of rebellious "outs" who could eventually be reabsorbed. When Hurley and Wedemeyer during this visit, along with Commodore M. E. Miles (Chief of Naval Intelligence in China), conferred with the Joint Chiefs, "they were all of the opinion," as reported by Admiral William D. Leahy, "that the rebellion in China could be put down by comparatively small assistance to Chiang's central government."

A second factor was that no proponent of another view, no one within the government who could effectively counter Hurley's version, had regular access to Roosevelt. This left a terrible gap. The President, again according to Leahy who lived in the White House, "had much confidence in Hurley's reliability in accurately carrying out the duties assigned to him in the foreign field." Moreover, if Leahy can be used as a mirror, the White House bought the thesis that Hurley was undermined in his efforts by a group of jealous career diplomats who had "ganged up on the new Ambassador appointed from outside the regular foreign service."

Here is a beam of light on the most puzzling aspect of our China policy: why the information and opinions provided by experienced observers maintained in the field for the express purpose of keeping our government informed were so consistently and regularly ignored.

The answer lies in the deep-seated American distrust that still prevailed of diplomacy and diplomats, the sentiment that disallowed knee-breeches for Americans. Diplomacy means all the wicked devices of the Old World, spheres of influence, balances of power, secret treaties, triple alliances, and, during the interwar period, appeasement of fascism. Roosevelt reflected the sentiment in his attitude toward the career Foreign Service, which he considered a group of striped-pants snobs drawn from the ranks of entrenched wealth (as many of them were), unrepresentative of America, and probably functioning as tools of the British.

There was enough truth in this picture to make it persist despite passage of the Rogers Act in 1924, formalizing the Foreign Service as a career based on entry by examination and promotion by merit. The Act itself had been the result of wide criticism of cliques in the State Department, leading to a congressional investigation. The tragedy was that Roosevelt's prejudice derived from his liberal instinct yet produced a quite astonishing rigidity. When the voice from the field reported evidence that interfered with his desire to believe, he assumed it was the voice of reaction. When officers of the Embassy in Moscow and of the Russian Division of the State Department (technically the Division of East European Affairs) reported critically and relentlessly the brutal truth of Stalin's purges of 1937, they spoiled an image and were accordingly judged to be a nest of reactionaries married to White Russian princesses. On orders from above, the Russian Division was abolished, its unique files destroyed, its library given over to the Library of Congress, and its chief, Robert F. Kelly, who had assembled over the years a collection of material that Litvinov envied, transferred to another post.

Ironically, the snob reputation had not on the whole been valid for China which, not being considered a particularly desirable post by socialites who preferred the Quai d'Orsay and the Court of St. James's, had been filled by academics, missionaries' sons, and hard-working men promoted from the consular service, like Johnson and Gauss, the two ambassadors preceding Hurley. By a double irony, just such men would not have found themselves on easy terms with the White House.

Hurley started his mission with his mind equally set against the Foreign Service. When he came to blame it for his troubles, he accused it alternately of conspiring to support Communism and of sucking the United States into a power bloc "on the side of colonial imperialism." In this odd coupling he was not unique. Robert Sherwood, when conferring with General MacArthur's staff in Manila, found a persecution complex at work which seemed to conceive of the War Department, the Joint Chiefs, and even the White House as under the domination of "Communists and British Imperialists."

Finally, the weight of domestic opinion on Roosevelt must be taken into account. If the hold of Chiang Kai-shek as the archetypal anti-Communist on American public opinion was such that his cause perverted American politics for a decade after the war, and if it has taken us twenty-seven years to untie the silver cord, and even yet we have not cut it loose, it can hardly have been easy for Roosevelt to untie it in 1945. Fear of Communism lay very close beneath the skin, so close that in his final speech of the campaign of 1944, Governor Dewey, the Republican candidate, charged that Communists as a small disciplined minority, acting through Sidney Hillman, had seized control of the American Labor movement, and "now . . . are seizing control of the New Deal through which they aim to control the Government of the United States." Roosevelt, said this disciplined and respectable lawyer, had auctioned control of the Democratic Party to the "highest bidder," i.e., Hillman and Earl Browder, in order to perpetuate himself in office. Through him Communism would destroy liberties, religion, and private property.

If a man like Dewey could resort to the tactics of the enormous lie and to a charge as reckless as any in the history of political campaigning, Roosevelt was politician enough to know how little would be needed to revive it. The autocrat of the *Time-Life* empire, Henry R. Luce, was rabid on this subject, especially with reference to China; his publications were the trumpet of Chiang's cause. Summoned to battle by Chiang's partisans, some of them sincere and passionate advocates like the former medical missionary, Congressman Walter Judd, any of the myriad enemies of the Administration could create serious trouble. Roosevelt was concentrating now on the coming conference in San Francisco to organize the United Nations and on his hopes of a four-power alliance after the war to keep world peace. It was a time at all costs to avoid friction. Since China was in any case secondary to Europe—a disability it suffered from all through the war—it did not seem worth the risk that the Atcheson telegram asked him to take.

Thus passed the opportunity Mao and Chou had asked for. The factors operating against it suggest there never was an "if." And yet, there remains one strange contradictory sliver of evidence. Edgar Snow, the kind of outsider from whom Roosevelt liked to get his facts, reported a conversation with the President in March 1945 at the very time of the Hurley-Wedemeyer visit. Roosevelt was "baffled yet acutely fascinated," Snow said, by the complexity of what was happening in China and complained that nobody explained it satisfactorily, Snow included. "He understood that our wartime aid was actually a form of intervention in China"; he "recognized the growing strength of the Chinese Communists as the effective government of the guerrilla area"; he asked "whether they were real

Communists and whether the Russians were boss-
ing them," and asked further, "what, concretely,
the Eighth Route Army could do with our aid in
North China. He then said that we were going to
land supplies and liaison officers on the North
China coast as we drew closer to Japan." Snow
questioned whether, so long as we recognized
Chiang Kai-shek as the sole government, all supplies would have to go through him. " 'We can't
support two governments in China, can we?' " he
asked.

" 'Well, I've been working with two governments there.' The President threw back his head
decisively, 'I intend to go on doing so until I can
get them together.' "

This is a puzzle. It seems irreconcilable with the
decision to uphold Hurley, unless Roosevelt was
so convinced that Hurley would indeed achieve
coalition "by the end of April" that what he had
in mind was sending the Communists arms and
aid *after* they had become part of the National
Government.

Of the major quirk in the case one has to ask
whether there might have been a different result
if the ambassador had been a different man. A different man could still not have achieved coalition
because no one on earth could have arranged
terms that both parties could accept. A different
man might have facilitated rather than blocked the
visit of Mao and Chou to Washington, but if he
had been a different man in whom they had con-

fidence, they would not have asked to go. There remains only the remote chance that an ambassador who both listened to his staff *and* had the ear of the President might have turned the President toward a wider option than the blank check to the Generalissimo.

Otherwise it would seem from the record that our course was destined, not by our stars but by ourselves and our inclinations; that the President, the public, and the conduct of foreign policy combined to work toward an inescapable and, from our point of view, a negative end.

VII

Is any principle contained in this dusty answer? Perhaps only that every revolutionary change exacts a price in loss as well as gain, and that history will continue to present us with problems for which there is no good and achievable solution. To insist that there is one and commit ourselves to it invites the fate set apart for hubris. We reached in China exactly the opposite of what had been our object. Civil war, the one absolute we tried to prevent, duly came about. Though we defeated Japan, the goal that would have made sense of the victory, a strong united China on our side after the war, escaped us. The entire effort predicated on the validity of the Nationalist government was wasted.

What should have been our aim in China was not to mediate or settle China's internal problem, which was utterly beyond our scope, but to preserve viable and as far as possible amicable relations with the government of China whatever it turned out to be. We were not compelled to make an either/or decision; we could have adopted the British attitude, described by Sir John Keswick as one of "slightly perplexed resignation." Or, as a Brookings Institution study concluded in 1956, the United States "could have considered its China policy at a dead stop and ended all further effort to direct the outcome of events."

Yet we repeat the pattern. An architect of our involvement in Vietnam, Walt Rostow, insists that a fundamental premise of American policy is the establishment of a stable balance of power in Asia. This is not a condition the West can establish. Stability in Asia is no more achievable by us than was unity in China in 1945.

Basic to the conduct of foreign policy is the problem basic to all policy: how to apply wisdom to government. If wisdom in government eludes us, perhaps courage could substitute—the moral courage to terminate mistakes.

Unanimous Acclaim for Barbara W. Tuchman's *Stilwell and the American Experience in China*

1911-45

WINNER 1972 PULITZER PRIZE

"An admirably structured work that is excellent as narrative and fascinating as history . . . of major importance for the reappraisal, now become essential, of our China policy—and of our Asian policy as a whole. . . . One sees striking parallels between the situation that existed in China during the Stilwell years and that in Southeast Asia today."

—O. Edmund Clubb
Saturday Review

"The most interesting and informative book on U.S.-China relations to appear since World War II . . . a brilliant, lucid and authentic account of a highly complicated subject that has too long lain buried under the political polemics of 'how China was lost.'"

—Allen S. Whiting
The Nation

"This book will be a major protagonist in the continuing controversy about China."

—John K. Fairbank
*Director, East Asian Research Center,
Harvard University*